Joyce Appleby on *Thomas Jefferson*
Louis Auchincloss on *Theodore Roosevelt*
Jean H. Baker on *James Buchanan*
H. W. Brands on *Woodrow Wilson*
Alan Brinkley on *John F. Kennedy*
Douglas Brinkley on *Gerald R. Ford*
Josiah Bunting III on *Ulysses S. Grant*
James MacGregor Burns and Susan Dunn on *George Washington*
Charles W. Calhoun on *Benjamin Harrison*
Gail Collins on *William Henry Harrison*
Robert Dallek on *Harry S. Truman*
John W. Dean on *Warren G. Harding*
John Patrick Diggins on *John Adams*
Elizabeth Drew on *Richard M. Nixon*
John S. D. Eisenhower on *Zachary Taylor*
Paul Finkelman on *Millard Fillmore*
Annette Gordon-Reed on *Andrew Johnson*
Henry F. Graff on *Grover Cleveland*
David Greenberg on *Calvin Coolidge*
Gary Hart on *James Monroe*
Michael F. Holt on *Franklin Pierce*
Roy Jenkins on *Franklin Delano Roosevelt*
Zachary Karabell on *Chester Alan Arthur*
Lewis H. Lapham on *William Howard Taft*
William E. Leuchtenburg on *Herbert Hoover*
James Mann on *George W. Bush*
Gary May on *John Tyler*
George McGovern on *Abraham Lincoln*
Timothy Naftali on *George H. W. Bush*
Charles Peters on *Lyndon B. Johnson*
Kevin Phillips on *William McKinley*
Robert V. Remini on *John Quincy Adams*
Ira Rutkow on *James A. Garfield*
John Seigenthaler on *James K. Polk*
Hans L. Trefousse on *Rutherford B. Hayes*
Tom Wicker on *Dwight D. Eisenhower*
Ted Widmer on *Martin Van Buren*
Sean Wilentz on *Andrew Jackson*
Garry Wills on *James Madison*
Julian E. Zelizer on *Jimmy Carter*

Millard Fillmore

Paul Finkelman

Millard Fillmore

THE AMERICAN PRESIDENTS

ARTHUR M. SCHLESINGER, JR., AND SEAN WILENTZ

GENERAL EDITORS

Times Books

HENRY HOLT AND COMPANY, NEW YORK

Times Books
Henry Holt and Company, LLC
Publishers since 1866
175 Fifth Avenue
New York, New York 10010
www.henryholt.com

Henry Holt® is a registered trademark of
Henry Holt and Company, LLC.

Copyright © 2011 by Paul Finkelman
All rights reserved.
Frontispiece: © Bettmann/CORBIS

Library of Congress Cataloging-in-Publication Data
Finkelman, Paul, 1949–
  Millard Fillmore / Paul Finkelman.
      p.   cm.—(The American presidents series)
  Includes bibliographical references and index.
  ISBN 978-0-8050-8715-4
  1. Fillmore, Millard, 1800–1874.   2. Presidents—United States—
Biography.   3. United States—Politics and government—1849–1853.
  I. Title.
  E427.F56 2011
  973.6'4092—dc22
  [B]   2010047174

Henry Holt books are available for special promotions and
premiums. For details contact: Director, Special Markets.

First Edition 2011

Printed in the United States of America
1   3   5   7   9   10   8   6   4   2

For Abraham R. Wagner,
a True Son of Buffalo

Contents

Editor's Note

THE AMERICAN PRESIDENCY

The president is the central player in the American political order. That would seem to contradict the intentions of the Founding Fathers. Remembering the horrid example of the British monarchy, they invented a separation of powers in order, as Justice Brandeis later put it, "to preclude the exercise of arbitrary power." Accordingly, they divided the government into three allegedly equal and coordinate branches—the executive, the legislative, and the judiciary.

But a system based on the tripartite separation of powers has an inherent tendency toward inertia and stalemate. One of the three branches must take the initiative if the system is to move. The executive branch alone is structurally capable of taking that initiative. The Founders must have sensed this when they accepted Alexander Hamilton's proposition in the Seventieth Federalist that "energy in the executive is a leading character in the definition of good government." They thus envisaged a strong president—but within an equally strong system of constitutional accountability. (The term *imperial presidency* arose in the 1970s to describe the situation when the balance between power and accountability is upset in favor of the executive.)

The American system of self-government thus comes to focus in the presidency—"the vital place of action in the system," as Woodrow Wilson put it. Henry Adams, himself the great-grandson and grandson of presidents as well as the most brilliant of American historians, said that the American president "resembles the commander of a ship at sea. He must have a helm to grasp, a course to steer, a port to seek." The men in the White House (thus far only men, alas) in steering their chosen courses have shaped our destiny as a nation.

Biography offers an easy education in American history, rendering the past more human, more vivid, more intimate, more accessible, more connected to ourselves. Biography reminds us that presidents are not supermen. They are human beings too, worrying about decisions, attending to wives and children, juggling balls in the air, and putting on their pants one leg at a time. Indeed, as Emerson contended, "There is properly no history; only biography."

Presidents serve us as inspirations, and they also serve us as warnings. They provide bad examples as well as good. The nation, the Supreme Court has said, has "no right to expect that it will always have wise and humane rulers, sincerely attached to the principles of the Constitution. Wicked men, ambitious of power, with hatred of liberty and contempt of law, may fill the place once occupied by Washington and Lincoln."

The men in the White House express the ideals and the values, the frailties and the flaws, of the voters who send them there. It is altogether natural that we should want to know more about the virtues and the vices of the fellows we have elected to govern us. As we know more about them, we will know more about ourselves. The French political philosopher Joseph de Maistre said, "Every nation has the government it deserves."

At the start of the twenty-first century, forty-two men have made it to the Oval Office. (George W. Bush is counted our forty-third president, because Grover Cleveland, who served nonconsecutive terms, is counted twice.) Of the parade of presidents, a dozen or so lead the polls periodically conducted by historians and political scientists. What makes a great president?

Great presidents possess, or are possessed by, a vision of an ideal America. Their passion, as they grasp the helm, is to set the ship of state on the right course toward the port they seek. Great presidents also have a deep psychic connection with the needs, anxieties, dreams of people. "I do not believe," said Wilson, "that any man can lead who does not act . . . under the impulse of a profound sympathy with those whom he leads—a sympathy which is insight—an insight which is of the heart rather than of the intellect."

"All of our great presidents," said Franklin D. Roosevelt, "were leaders of thought at a time when certain ideas in the life of the nation had to be clarified." So Washington incarnated the idea of federal union, Jefferson and Jackson the idea of democracy, Lincoln union and freedom, Cleveland rugged honesty. Theodore Roosevelt and Wilson, said FDR, were both "moral leaders, each in his own way and his own time, who used the presidency as a pulpit."

To succeed, presidents not only must have a port to seek but they must convince Congress and the electorate that it is a port worth seeking. Politics in a democracy is ultimately an educational process, an adventure in persuasion and consent. Every president stands in Theodore Roosevelt's bully pulpit.

The greatest presidents in the scholars' rankings, Washington, Lincoln, and Franklin Roosevelt, were leaders who confronted and overcame the republic's greatest crises. Crisis widens presidential opportunities for bold and imaginative action. But it does not guarantee presidential greatness. The crisis of secession did not spur Buchanan or the crisis of depression spur Hoover to creative leadership. Their inadequacies in the face of crisis allowed Lincoln and the second Roosevelt to show the difference individuals make to history. Still, even in the absence of first-order crisis, forceful and persuasive presidents—Jefferson, Jackson, James K. Polk, Theodore Roosevelt, Harry Truman, John F. Kennedy, Ronald Reagan, George W. Bush— are able to impose their own priorities on the country.

The diverse drama of the presidency offers a fascinating set of tales. Biographies of American presidents constitute a chronicle of wisdom and folly, nobility and pettiness, courage and cunning, forthrightness and deceit, quarrel and consensus. The turmoil perennially swirling around the White House illuminates the heart of the American democracy.

It is the aim of the American Presidents series to present the grand panorama of our chief executives in volumes compact enough for the busy reader, lucid enough for the student, authoritative enough for the scholar. Each volume offers a distillation of character and career. I hope that these lives will give readers some understanding of the pitfalls and potentialities of the presidency and also of the responsibilities of citizenship. Truman's famous sign—"The buck stops here"—tells only half the story. Citizens cannot escape the ultimate responsibility. It is in the voting booth, not on the presidential desk, that the buck finally stops.

—Arthur M. Schlesinger, Jr.

Millard Fillmore

1

Portrait of a Young Man from Nowhere

The president's death caught the nation by surprise. At sixty-five Zachary Taylor had been one of the oldest men elected to the office, but he was strong and hardy. A lifelong soldier, he had led armies and endured combat in snowy Midwest forests, steamy Florida swamps, and, most recently, in ovenlike Southwestern deserts. Taylor had fought the British, the Mexicans, and numerous Indian nations. "Old Rough and Ready," as his troops affectionately called him, was a tough soldier. Who would have imagined that just sixteen months into his term he would die from gastroenteritis—a massive stomachache? There were rumors that Taylor had been poisoned, and in the most literal sense that was probably true. The gastroenteritis may have killed him, but it is just as likely the hero of the Mexican War died from the treatment of his physicians in the age of "heroic medicine." His doctors bled him, put blisters on him, and gave him massive doses of calomel, a mercury compound that is indeed poisonous. Either way, the end result was the death of a popular and tough president on July 9, 1850. For the second time in the nation's history, an "accidental president" would take the oath of office.[1]

Taylor's presidency and death were weirdly similar to the only other president who had died in office, William Henry Harrison, who had served for just one month in 1841. Popular generals and war heroes, both were well past sixty when they were elected. Both were Whigs—the only candidates of that party ever to have been elected to the presidency. Both were southern-born slave owners, although Harrison had relocated to Ohio as a relatively young man.[2] However, the background and stature of the men who replaced each deceased president were completely dissimilar. John Tyler, Harrison's vice president, who became the first accidental president, was a significant figure. His wealthy father had been governor of Virginia. After graduating from the College of William and Mary, Tyler began his long prepresidential career at age twenty-one when he was elected to the state legislature. He later served as a congressman, governor, and U.S. senator, and he was elected president pro tempore of the Senate. When he was offered the vice presidential nomination in 1840, he was nationally prominent.

Millard Fillmore, who became president after Taylor's death, was inexperienced and virtually unknown when he was nominated for vice president at the 1848 Whig convention. He was born in poverty in central New York, poorly schooled as a child, and largely self-educated after that. He achieved a comfortable middle-class status and struggled to fit in with men who were better educated, culturally more sophisticated, and more socially adept than he. Moving to Buffalo, he practiced law and entered politics at age twenty-eight, serving three terms in the state legislature and later four terms in Congress. He was an unsuccessful candidate for governor of New York in 1844, but in 1847 he was elected state comptroller—an important but hardly a major office. A year later, this obscure politician was nominated to run for vice president alongside General Taylor.

Fillmore's presidency would be much like Tyler's. He is remembered as a thoroughly unsuccessful president who catered to the South at the expense of the North and energetically favored slavery over liberty. He alienated the party that nominated him for the vice presidency and, in the end, abandoned his party. The second accidental president, like the first, was a failure. Tyler left office rejected by his party. The same is true for Fillmore, except he also left office vilified in much of his home state and region. The final political ventures of both accidental presidents added no luster to their memory. Tyler's political career ended disgracefully. A man who had taken an oath "to preserve, protect and defend the Constitution of the United States"[3] turned traitor, accepted a position in the Confederate government, and helped make war on the nation he once led. Fillmore's career did not end in treason, but it is hardly praiseworthy. Desperate to regain the presidency, in 1856 he ran as the candidate of the anti-immigrant, anti-Catholic American Party—better known as the Know-Nothings. His campaign as the candidate of ethnic and religious bigotry ended in abysmal failure; he carried only one state, Maryland, which ironically had been founded in the seventeenth century as a haven for Catholics.

After his defeat as the Know-Nothing presidential candidate, Fillmore devoted his life to charity, local public service, and personal comfort, and until the Civil War he kept out of politics. Following the death of his first wife, he remarried a wealthy widow, and he spent the last eighteen years of his life basking in the glow of being a former president. To his credit, he supported the Union cause at the beginning of the Civil War, raised some money for war relief, and even organized a unit of aging men to serve as a more or less symbolic home guard. But the former president failed to follow most of his Whig contemporaries into the Republican Party. In 1864 he backed the Democratic candidate, George B. McClellan, once again supporting appeasement of the South and slavery. Like McClellan, Fillmore opposed emancipation, the enlistment of black troops, and expanding racial equality. Out of step with his neighbors, his former Whig allies, and the North, he became politically irrelevant. After the Civil War, he engaged in civic enterprises and boosterism for his adopted home of Buffalo, New York, where he died in 1874, forgotten by most of the nation and remembered, if at all, for his odd first name and his failed presidency.

Yet for a short moment, from July 1850 until March 1853, Millard Fillmore sat in the White House, at the center of American politics. His term coincided with one of the great crises of American history, and his leadership, or lack thereof, did little to either solve the nation's problems or reduce its tensions. Indeed, his presidency exacerbated both.

·   ·   ·

The first son of Nathaniel and Phoebe Fillmore, the future president was born on January 7, 1800, on an isolated farm at the southern end of Cayuga County, New York, west of present-day Syracuse.[4] His unusual first name was his mother's maiden name, a common practice among New Englanders, which the Fillmores had been until 1799, when they gave up farming the rocky soil of Vermont in the belief that central New York offered better land and more opportunity. Their faith was misplaced. The soil was poor, the winters were harsh, and they lost the land they purchased because of an inadequate survey and uncertain titles. The Fillmores then rented a farm in the nearby village of Sempronius, on Lake Skaneateles, about twenty-five miles from Auburn, where Fillmore's chief rival in New York politics, William H. Seward, would begin his career. Renting, rather than owning, land was a huge decline in social status for the Fillmores in a community where independence and self-respect were tied to land ownership.

It was in Sempronius that Millard learned to farm and gained a rudimentary education in the local elementary school. Nathaniel Fillmore, hoping for a better future for his son, apprenticed Millard to learn the trade of wool carding and cloth dressing. Over the next four years, Millard worked as an apprentice in a textile mill, where he also did some bookkeeping. At seventeen Millard paid to join a new private library and began reading voraciously. In 1819, with the mill temporarily closed (perhaps from the fallout of the financial panic that year), Millard enrolled in a recently opened local academy, where he was introduced to new fields of knowledge. He also met his future wife Abigail Powers, a teacher in the school. She was two years his senior, the daughter of a deceased Baptist minister and the sister of a local judge. Abigail was well read and as sophisticated as one could become at the time in a tiny town in rural central New York. At about this time Nathaniel Fillmore persuaded a county judge, Walter Wood, to take in Millard as a law clerk. Two months into his legal education the mill reopened.

Throughout this period Fillmore was legally still apprenticed to the mill, so he was technically required to return to the textile factory. Judge Wood wanted Fillmore to remain, lending him money and promising some paid work if he would stay. Fillmore continued to live at home, taught school, used his earnings to buy his way out of his apprenticeship at the mill, and returned to Judge Wood. However, reading the law and clerking under the autocratic judge soon became unbearable, while the pittance Wood paid him left Fillmore impoverished. About eighteen months after he returned to read the law under Wood, Fillmore accepted a few dollars to represent someone in a case before a justice of the peace. Fillmore needed the extra money, and by successfully negotiating a settlement before the case was heard, he hoped Judge Wood would not find out what he had done. Although admission to the bar was not required to practice law before a justice of the peace, it was clearly inappropriate for a law clerk to freelance in this way without the permission of the lawyer for whom he worked. Wood soon discovered this insubordination and properly reprimanded his clerk. The headstrong young Fillmore stormed off and returned to his father's farm. Shortly after, the entire Fillmore family moved to East Aurora, near Buffalo. Millard taught school again and argued a few more justice of the peace cases. Six feet tall, strikingly handsome, and ambitious for a better life, Millard Fillmore turned twenty-one with few prospects. He and Abigail announced their engagement, but she remained with her mother, teaching school in Cayuga County.

Fillmore, now of legal majority and emancipated from his father, was free to strike out on his own. He moved to Buffalo, where he once again taught school and found an attorney under whom he could read the law. He was meticulously dressed, well spoken, and clearly smart. He was orthodox in his thinking and circumspect in his politics. If he had any ideals, no one knew what they were, but he was generally cautious, conservative, serious, studious, and hard-working. In his first year clerking in Buffalo, Fillmore so impressed members of the local bar that they secured his early admission, allowing him to practice at the age of twenty-three.

Fillmore rejected offers to join existing Buffalo practices and returned to East Aurora, where he was the only attorney in town. His small-town legal work—wills, real estate, debt collection— allowed him to earn a decent living and teach himself how to practice law. It was a curious choice, since he would have learned more quickly if he had stayed on as a junior attorney in Buffalo, where he had read law. But after years of apprenticeships and being under the thumb of older men, the young lawyer must have relished being his own boss, especially in a town where there were no competing attorneys. Late in life, Fillmore would explain that he chose this route because he lacked the self-confidence to practice in Buffalo.

This insecurity reflected his impoverished youth, poor education, and the status decline of his family when they lost their land. He was a poor boy from the sticks. His father was an unsuccessful farmer. He had only a year or two of formal education beyond the rudimentary elementary schools of Cayuga County. He was well read and always striving to appear better read, but his education lacked any intellectual rigor. Throughout his life he was a consumer of books so that he could constantly educate himself. He was always impeccably dressed—perhaps the sign of a pretender trying to convince those around him that he actually belonged in polite society. He was, and always would be, cautious and conservative in his demeanor and style. Even in his personal life he must have been plagued by insecurities. It is true that he was a very handsome young man, but he was in love with a beautiful woman who came from a prominent, well-educated, and comparatively sophisticated family. He was the son of a dirt farmer, a self-educated factory apprentice who had somehow become a lawyer.

In many ways Fillmore's life mirrors that of the other famous frontier president of this period, Abraham Lincoln. Both were from poor farm families, were largely self-educated, and became successful lawyers. But their differences and their ideological developments are more important than their similarities. As a boy Fillmore attended local public schools while working on the farm and found time to gain more education while apprenticed at the mill. His father wanted him to succeed, supported his educational strivings, found him his first law clerkship, and encouraged him all along the way. Fillmore had a loving and apparently emotionally comfortable home with two supportive parents. It was a home he could return to throughout his youth and young adulthood, even after he was admitted to the bar. In contrast, Lincoln's mother died when he was a child, and he had to struggle against a tyrannical father to gain an education. Growing up in rural Kentucky and Indiana, he had virtually no formal schooling, and his father discouraged him from getting any. Lincoln's father thought reading was a waste of time and a sign of laziness. While Fillmore returned home after being admitted to the bar, Lincoln could not wait to leave home at age twenty-one, and once gone he never looked back.

The relationship of both men to politics is also revealing. Lincoln—a "little engine of ambition," as his law partner William Herndon called him—was always engaged in politics. He ran for public office before he married, secured a profession, or had a steady income. He became a lawyer after he was elected to office, and while his legal career made him economically comfortable, politics motivated him. Fillmore's approach to law and politics—and to life itself—was more plodding. He came to politics opportunistically, almost by accident, rather than by design. He might have happily remained a successful lawyer and civic leader in Buffalo. Lincoln hungered for more.

Equally intriguing is the contrast in their striving for social success and acceptability. The well-dressed Fillmore was perpetually conscious of his manners and public persona. He was a parvenu who seemed always worried that someone might discover he did not belong in proper society. He changed churches as he became more successful and moved to bigger and better houses. Outward appearances truly mattered to him. Lincoln was a rawboned frontier lawyer and politician. Until he ran for president, he showed little interest in his clothing or his appearance. Ambitious as he was, he did not pretend to be pious and was never a churchgoer. Lincoln was famous for his sense of humor and his ribald jokes. It is impossible to imagine the dour Fillmore telling a joke, much less an off-color one.

Both men were Whigs, and both were devoted to the Union and the Constitution. But Fillmore was drawn to oddball political movements, conspiracy theories, and ethnic hatred. Whether opportunistically or out of conviction, Fillmore launched his political career as an Anti-Mason in the 1820s. When the Anti-Masonic movement ran its course, he became a traditional Whig but easily trafficked with anti-Catholic and anti-immigrant groups. Significantly, Fillmore's rivals in the New York Whig Party, William H. Seward and Thurlow Weed, opposed any bargain with the nativists because it would simultaneously "weaken the party's integrity and alienate immigrants."[5] Fillmore was always comfortable with nativists and utterly oblivious to the concerns of immigrants and religious minorities, just as he had no concern for the plight of fugitive slaves or the rights of free blacks. As president, he would push for ratification of a treaty with Switzerland that discriminated against Jewish Americans, and in 1856 he would try to relaunch his career as the presidential candidate of the anti-Catholic, anti-immigrant Know-Nothing Party. Lincoln, by contrast, was happy to have the Know-Nothings' support and welcomed them into the Republican Party, but he never supported their anti-immigrant or anti-Catholic goals and never offered them any support. As he told Joshua Speed, "I am not a Know-Nothing. That is certain. How could I be? How can any one who abhors the oppression of negroes, be in favor of degrading classes of white people?" As a politician in Illinois, he worked closely with Germans, like Gustav Koerner, and praised them while campaigning.[6] Indeed, as president, Lincoln was careful to seek out ethnic generals and advisers, and he famously countermanded General Ulysses S. Grant's ill-considered General Order No. 11, which had banned Jews from his military district.[7] Lincoln appeared incapable of judging a man by his faith or ethnicity. Fillmore never had such scruples.

The most important contrast between the two concerns how work and servitude as young men affected their views as adults. By age eighteen, Lincoln was ready to strike out on his own, to earn his own living and continue on his lifelong course of reading and self-education. Under the law, he could not leave home until he turned twenty-one without his father's permission, which Thomas Lincoln would not grant. Lincoln always saw these last years of his legal "childhood" as a kind of indentured servitude that mirrored the bondage of black slaves, which he saw on his famous rafting trip down the Mississippi. At twenty-one the emancipated Lincoln permanently left his father's house. Lincoln's profound antipathy to slavery—he would famously write, "if slavery is not wrong then nothing is wrong"[8]—stemmed in part from his own experience in a kind of temporary bondage from which there was no escape until he came of age. In sharp contrast, Fillmore strongly supported the Fugitive Slave Act of 1850, which was designed to prevent slaves from gaining their own liberty, even when, through their own ingenuity, they managed the arduous task of escaping to the North.

Slavery would be the central issue in the political lives of both men, but their responses were dramatically different. In the end, Fillmore was prepared to give the South whatever it wanted to protect slavery, at whatever cost. Lincoln, who never compromised on stopping the spread of slavery before his presidency and never compromised on ending slavery after 1863, was always willing to negotiate with the South, but he never backed away from his core principles. Lincoln never deviated from his "oft-expressed *personal* wish that all men every where could be free."[9] Fillmore had no such wish.

· · ·

As a young lawyer in East Aurora, Fillmore built a respectable practice, purchased and read all the law books he could find (to overcome his lack of a full legal apprenticeship), and, most important, reunited with Abigail. He had left Cayuga County on foot with few prospects, but he returned by carriage, an impeccably dressed, tall, handsome young lawyer, who appeared to be on the cusp of a successful career. In February 1826 Abigail and Millard were married by an Episcopal priest, a social step up from his moderate Methodist background and the Baptist tradition of Abigail's late father. For Fillmore, a young man on the make, his new social status required a more elite church. The newlyweds returned to East Aurora, where Abigail continued to teach for two years. This made her the only first lady before the twentieth century to have worked outside the home after her marriage.[10] Her employment after marriage also suggests that while Fillmore was rising in his profession, he was hardly economically secure at this time.

Shortly after his marriage, Fillmore took in his first law clerk, Nathan K. Hall. This signaled not only his emerging economic success—he could afford to hire someone to work in his office—but also his professional accomplishment. Fillmore now felt secure enough as a lawyer to train others for the profession. Bringing in Hall also indicated that Fillmore had enough work to need the assistance of an apprentice. By 1831 Hall would become his law partner and would remain Fillmore's confidant and ally for the rest of their lives.

In 1824 Fillmore had supported John Quincy Adams in the presidential election, but otherwise he was far too busy with his legal career to be involved with politics. This changed with the emergence of the Anti-Masonic Party in 1827, an odd and short-lived political movement that was mostly part of a larger scheme to help defeat Andrew Jackson, who had lost to Adams in 1824 but was running against him in 1828. The movement was initially centered in western New York and was particularly strong in rural Erie County, where Fillmore lived. The party developed in response to the disappearance of William Morgan, a local stonemason who was said to have been murdered by members of the Masonic Order because he was going to reveal the organization's secrets. The reaction to Morgan's disappearance fueled resentment of this secret order, and this played into the hands of supporters of John Quincy Adams and opponents of the emerging Democratic Party in New York State (many of whose leaders were Masons) and their hero Andrew Jackson (who was also a Mason). As passions grew, Fillmore was drawn to the movement against this alleged giant Masonic conspiracy.

In many ways, Fillmore's attraction to Anti-Masonry is consistent with his later associations with the anti-immigrant and anti-Catholic North American Party in the 1840s and the Know-Nothing Party in the 1850s and his deep hostility to abolitionists during the same period. Fillmore saw conspiracies, or at least dangers to the body politic and the American Union, as he envisioned it, from outsiders—Catholics, immigrants, abolitionists who questioned the status quo, or fugitive slaves who rejected the conditions of their birth. Fear of a secret society like the Masons fit into this worldview and dovetailed with Fillmore's conservative, rural, Protestant background. However, in other ways Fillmore's interests and goals were unlike those of the core of the Anti-Masonic Party. Most Anti-Masons were egalitarian, objecting to the exclusiveness of a secret society, but Fillmore was always striving to be included among the better classes. Many Anti-Masons, including William H. Seward in New York and Thaddeus Stevens in Pennsylvania, would later emerge as staunch opponents of slavery. The moralistic, reformist element of Anti-Masonry would reemerge as "the antislavery 'Conscience' wing" of the Whig Party.[11] These Conscience Whigs would eventually become the core of the Republican Party. But Fillmore was not moralistic in this way. He would never be outraged by slavery and would never lift a finger in opposition to its spread. His affiliation with the Anti-Masons was not, in the end, about moral reform. Rather, it appears that for Fillmore the Anti-Masonic movement was a comfortable vehicle to move into politics.[12]

Drawn into the Anti-Masonic movement and deeply opposed to the Jacksonian Democrats in Albany and Washington, Fillmore became a natural leader in East Aurora. In quick order he was chosen as a delegate to Erie County's National Republican Convention (the National Republicans were the forerunners of the Whigs), which endorsed John Quincy Adams for another term as president,

and then in July 1828 he was a delegate at two separate Anti-
Masonic conventions. The young lawyer discovered that he liked
the political negotiations, and in September he was nominated for
the state assembly on a coalition ticket of National Republicans and
Anti-Masons. In November he was swept into office.

Fillmore served three successive terms in the New York Assembly, learning how legislatures operated and how politics worked. In
his final term, he sponsored legislation to abolish imprisonment for
debt in New York. Success depended on persuading the Democratic majority to support the bill. Such a bill was consistent with
the Jacksonian goal of rationalizing criminal law. Almost everyone
believed that imprisonment for debt made no logical sense since
someone in jail could hardly earn money to pay his creditors. The
practice was a holdover from an earlier period in England when
debtors were almost always men of the upper classes who were
believed to be concealing assets to avoid their debts. This was
surely not the case in Jacksonian America, when debt was common
and insolvents were often casualties of economic downturns like
the Panic of 1819 (and later the Panic of 1837). But in this highly
partisan age, the Democrats in Albany were unlikely to support a
bill sponsored by an Anti-Mason. Shrewdly, Fillmore effectively
withdrew as the sponsor of the bill, allowing the Democrats to take
credit for an important package of reforms. The new laws ended
imprisonment for debt, allowed for the discharge of debts through
personal bankruptcy, and criminalized fraudulent bankruptcy.
These new laws would help unleash the expanding New York economy while protecting creditors and debtors alike. It was a crowning
achievement to Fillmore's three terms in the legislature, showing
that he could negotiate across the aisle and be a true reformer. The
new laws also reflected Fillmore's growing interest in finance and
economic policy and his strong support for business interests. The
abolition of imprisonment for debt and the new bankruptcy laws
were helpful to all New Yorkers, but these laws were especially
helpful to entrepreneurs and businessmen, part of the core con-
stituency that had supported John Quincy Adams.

In 1830 Fillmore moved to Buffalo, and when his one-year term in the state legislature was up in 1831 he declined to run again, since he no longer lived in the East Aurora district that he had represented. Instead, he settled into a comfortable role as an increasingly prominent lawyer and a civic booster. He served on civic and corporate boards, was an officer in the local lyceum, and joined the Unitarian Church, which was the denomination of choice for well-off, educated Protestants, particularly those with a New England background who were more interested in moral and civic virtue than faith, piety, or theology. At the terminus of the Erie Canal, Buffalo had a promising future, and Fillmore would live through most of it. When he arrived in the city, it had just over eight thousand residents. By 1860 Fillmore's adopted hometown would be the tenth-largest city in the nation with more than eighty thousand inhabitants.

In 1832 Fillmore was back in politics, winning a seat in Congress with a party affiliation that is uncertain. He was nominally still an Anti-Mason, but the party was dying and Fillmore no longer needed this fringe party for his political success. During this term in the House of Representatives, he became a solid supporter of the Whig Party and a protégé of Senator Daniel Webster of Massachusetts, who sponsored Fillmore when he was sworn in as a member of the bar of the U.S. Supreme Court. This was not much of an accomplishment—any lawyer with enough years of practice could be admitted to the Supreme Court Bar if sponsored by an existing member. But to have Webster sponsor him was an honor. Admission to the Supreme Court Bar would also make him seem even more important when he returned to Buffalo and thus enhance his law practice. Doubtless, the still unsophisticated and insecure young congressman from the western edge of New York State was delighted and flattered that the great Webster would share meals with him and help him learn the ropes in Washington. Webster, on the other hand, understood that extending his patronage to young congressmen like Fillmore would gain him support for his own life-long quest for the presidency. This connection would continue until Webster's death in 1852.

Despite this connection to Webster, Fillmore did not seek reelection in 1834. After his term he withdrew from the Anti-Masons but refused a Whig nomination, correctly believing that if he ran as a Whig and the Anti-Masons also ran a candidate, it would only ensure a victory for a Jacksonian Democrat. He might have accepted the nomination of both parties, but this did not happen. Fillmore also may have been deeply ambivalent about returning to Washington, while leaving his wife and baby daughter back in Buffalo. Instead, he went back to law practice and local political maneuvering. Fillmore was thoroughly engaged in Whig politics, rivaling William H. Seward for leadership in the state party. In 1836 Seward lost as the Whig candidate for governor but came back to win the office in 1838 and again in 1840. Meanwhile, Fillmore, now running as a Whig, was elected to Congress in 1836, 1838, and 1840. In his last term, he was the runner-up to be Speaker of the House and ended up as chairman of the powerful House Ways and Means Committee.

As chair of Ways and Means, Fillmore was able to prevent a reduction of the existing tariff rates, which was set to take place. This was a key part of the Whig program, and on economic policy Fillmore was a thoroughly orthodox Whig. Fillmore argued it was necessary to keep the tariff at the existing rate to prevent the national government from a severe financial crisis. This was true, but the final tariff bill that Fillmore guided through Congress was hugely protective, with rates averaging 30 percent and some rates as high as 50 percent. The tariff on imported bar iron increased to 85 percent. The higher tariff raised Fillmore's stature with other Whigs and also benefited Fillmore's business and manufacturing constituents in Buffalo, which had grown to nearly twenty thousand people by 1840. In the wake of this legislative success and his new prestige among other Whigs in Congress, Fillmore chose not to run for another term. He was tired of Washington life and believed he could do more for the Whig Party and his own career back home in New York. Thus, in the summer of 1842 he announced he would not run for reelection in what was clearly a safe seat.

By this time Fillmore was involved in an ongoing struggle with

Seward and Thurlow Weed for control of the New York Whig Party. Their differences were political, ideological, and ultimately personal. As governor from 1839 to 1843, Seward had been deeply sympathetic to the abolitionists, who wanted New York to take a more aggressive stand against slavery. Seward had supported repeal of a 1799 law that allowed visiting southerners to bring their slaves into the state for up to nine months. The 1841 repeal of the Nine Months Law was an important victory for the antislavery wing of the Whig Party. Seward's role in the repeal put New York in the forefront of free states no longer willing to cooperate with slavery except when absolutely required to do so by the United States Constitution. After 1841 if a master brought a slave to New York, the slave would be instantly free. (In 1852, while Fillmore was president, a New York court freed eight Virginia slaves who had been locked up in a hotel room for the night as their owners changed ships to head south; in 1860 the highest court in New York upheld this result in *Lemmon v. The People*.)[13]

Similarly, Governor Seward refused to arrest three black New York merchant seamen indicted in Virginia for helping a slave to escape on their ship. Seward simply told the Virginians that New York did not recognize property in human beings; thus the three sailors could not be extradited for theft because they had not stolen anything. When successive Virginia governors complained, Seward brilliantly threw states' rights arguments in their faces, asserting that they surely agreed the states had a right to decide for themselves what their local laws would be. The New York–Virginia controversy complicated relations between the two states for nearly four years, but eventually the Virginians accepted Seward's states' rights arguments and dropped the matter.

These two issues solidified Seward as a staunch opponent of slavery and a friend of the abolitionists.[14] In this way he was dramatically different from his rival in Buffalo. Fillmore conventionally disliked slavery, as almost all northerners did, but he saw no reason to politicize the issue. Nor did he ever show any sympathy for slaves. Fillmore believed that the repeal of the Nine Months

Law unnecessarily exacerbated sectional tensions. He was willing to tolerate southerners bringing slaves into the state in order to ensure sectional harmony (and promote business with the South), just as he would have extradited the black sailors to Virginia for helping a slave escape. These views would be reflected throughout his career. Fillmore, who was as conservative in his politics as he was in his lifestyle, wanted nothing to do with the abolitionists and wanted the Whig Party to avoid any controversy over slavery.

Fillmore also disagreed with Seward on issues involving Catholics and immigrants. Since the state required that all children attend schools, the growing Catholic population in New York wanted state support for parochial schools. Fillmore was unalterably opposed to any government support for religious schools, couching his argument on traditional notions of separation of church and state. Such an argument may resonate well in the modern world, but Fillmore's notion of "separation" of church and state is deeply inconsistent with modern notions of the concept. At the time all children in New York's public schools participated in daily Bible readings and prayers, always using a Protestant translation of the Bible and reciting Protestant prayers. Thus, while claiming to favor "separation," what Fillmore actually favored was Protestant orthodoxy in public education. Seward, by contrast, was sympathetic to the claims of immigrants and Catholics that the New York public schools discriminated against them by forcing their children to read the Protestant Bible.[15]

•   •   •

In 1844 Fillmore sought the Whig nomination for vice president. He believed he could add to the ticket in a variety of ways. The new tariff would be an issue in the campaign. Whigs loved the tariff while most Democrats hated it. Fillmore could be an articulate defender of the tariff because he had helped guide it through Congress, and as a New Yorker he could help carry the nation's largest state as well as neighboring Pennsylvania, where manufacturing interests supported the tariff.

Fillmore believed he could also help balance the ticket on three interrelated issues: westward expansion, slavery, and the character and reputation of Henry Clay, who ultimately won the Whig nomination by acclamation at the party's convention. Clay had been a major figure in American politics for decades and was revered by many Whigs for his role in drafting the Missouri Compromise and guiding it through Congress in 1820. He was a slaveholder but managed to project an image of being moderately opposed to slavery. He was a longtime member of the American Colonization Society (ACS), which advocated sending all free blacks to Africa. Over its history, the ACS also facilitated freedom for about six thousand slaves, whose masters voluntarily manumitted them on condition that the ACS would take them to Liberia. This hardly dented the slave population, which would reach 3.9 million by the eve of the Civil War.

Abolitionists and almost all northern black activists hated the ACS. They considered it racist and hostile to the interests of slaves and free blacks. Conversely, extreme pro-slavery men considered the ACS to be a stalking horse of abolition, but this was absurdly wrong: most of the ACS leaders were slaveholders. Many conservatives in the South saw it as a way of ridding the nation of free blacks, while northern conservatives naively saw it as a vehicle for peaceably ending slavery. Many northern Whigs assumed that their antislavery neighbors would support Clay because he was more moderate on slavery than his Democratic opponent, the vigorously pro-slavery James K. Polk of Tennessee. Fillmore, from the antislavery heart of New York, thought he could help attract these voters, even though Fillmore himself had never taken any strong stand on slavery.

In addition to slaveholding, Clay's "character" was an issue for some Whigs. He seemed too smooth and slippery as a politician and, in other ways, unsavory to the evangelical Protestants who formed the bulk of the northern wing of the party. As the historian Michael Holt has noted, even before he gained the nomination, "Democrats were flaying Clay as a drunkard, gambler, profligate, and blasphemer."[16] Clay had also fought in at least one duel, which struck many Whigs, especially in the North, as barbaric and uncivilized. Democrats, even in the North, were careful not to remind northern Whigs that Clay was a slaveholder, because Polk was one as well. The northern Democrats could count on the explicitly antislavery Liberty Party to do that and possibly siphon off antislavery Whig votes.

The issue of slavery was directly tied to the question of expansion and Texas annexation. The Democrats were committed to the annexation of Texas as well as to a confrontation with Great Britain over the northwestern boundary of the United States. Under the slogan Fifty-Four Forty or Fight, Polk campaigned on the promise of forcing Britain to cede virtually all of present-day British Columbia to the United States. Whigs believed Polk's aggressive stance would lead to a war with Britain or Mexico, or both.

Almost all Whigs believed that annexation of Texas was unconstitutional. They also opposed annexation because the assumption of the debt of the Texas Republic would vastly increase the national debt. Most important, the Whigs understood (correctly, as it would turn out) that annexation would lead to a war with Mexico. Concerns over slavery led to Whig opposition from both sections of the country as well. In the South, Whigs argued that annexation would harm slavery because a large migration to Texas would raise the price of slaves and lower the price of land in the rest of the South. Most northern Whigs saw Texas annexation as a plot to spread slavery and to bring a new slave state into the Union. If Texas came into the Union, it would not only add another slave state but provide a vast empire of land where masters could bring their slaves. Northern Whigs, joined by some northern Democrats, saw Texas as a great "Empire for Slavery," and that was reason enough for them to oppose annexation. In Congress, the Whigs had blocked Texas annexation, with southern Whigs joining their northern colleagues, along with some northern Democrats who opposed Texas annexation because of slavery.

With these issues looming for the 1844 election, Fillmore hoped to be the vice presidential nominee. His campaign for the nomination rested on four prongs. First, the presumptive (and eventual) presidential nominee, Henry Clay of Kentucky, needed to run with a northerner to balance the ticket. Fillmore, a prominent Whig in the largest state of the Union, could surely offer that geographic balance. Although nominally opposed to slavery, Fillmore had never taken a public stand on the issue, had never associated with abolitionists, and had never used his legal talents to protect free blacks or fugitive slaves. New York abolitionists were not close to Fillmore, and he was surely no William H. Seward, who had aggressively fought slavery while governor. But Fillmore undoubtedly thought this worked in his favor. Fillmore was a northerner and that (he believed) made him antislavery enough to balance the ticket for Clay. He would provide sectional balance to the ticket by presumably being acceptable to the southern wing of the party because he was not openly antislavery. Fillmore had just served three successful terms in the House, where he had been one of the party leaders, although certainly not *the* party leader. In Congress, he had been a key supporter of the tariff bill and was deeply committed to other Whig programs on banking, currency, and bankruptcy. Finally, Fillmore believed he had the support of Seward and his chief ally, the editor Thurlow Weed, in his quest for the nomination.

Most of Fillmore's assumptions proved to be weak or just incorrect. A northerner had to balance the ticket, but Fillmore was not the right man. Fillmore had grown up in the heart of New York's antislavery "Burned-over District,"[17] and southerners, who did not really know his deeply conservative views on slavery, mistakenly assumed that he was antislavery. In the House, he had supported the right to present antislavery petitions to Congress, as had almost all northern Whigs. While he personally disliked slavery and thought it politically problematic, he had never taken a public stand on the issue. He opposed Texas annexation but not on antislavery grounds. Thus, he stood somewhere between Seward, who was open in his hatred of slavery and prepared to make policy accordingly, and former senator Theodore Frelinghuysen of New Jersey, who as a member of the American Colonization Society (like Clay) was clearly an opponent of the abolitionists. Fillmore would eventually support colonization, but no one knew this in 1844. Fillmore's service in Congress was exemplary, but he was only a former four-term congressman who was still virtually unknown outside of New York. Most important, Fillmore misunderstood the support he had from Seward and Weed. By this time Seward had his eye on the White House, and promoting Fillmore to the national stage would not play into that strategy. Seward and Weed gave tacit support to Fillmore and promised that if he did not get the vice presidential nomination, they would support him for governor. This fit better with their own goals. Fillmore was a plausible candidate for governor—a proven vote getter from the fast-growing western part of the state. Seward had already served two terms in that office, and helping regain it for the Whigs by being the kingmaker for Fillmore would enhance his prestige in the party. And if Fillmore failed to win the race, then he might be eliminated as a rival within the state. Weed and Seward gave Fillmore only nominal support for the vice presidential nomination at the national convention, but even their enthusiastic support probably would not have changed the result.

Why Fillmore thought he could gain the vice presidential nomination in 1844—or indeed why he did gain it four years later—remains something of a mystery. Since John Adams first held the office, every vice president had been a significant politician at the state or national level before gaining the nomination. Indeed, every vice president had been a state governor, a U.S. senator, a cabinet member, or a leading founder. John Adams and Thomas Jefferson were both signers of the Declaration of Independence and leaders of the Revolution. Elbridge Gerry (who was famous for inventing the gerrymander to manipulate electoral districts) had signed the Declaration of Independence, had been a delegate to the Constitutional Convention, and had served as governor of Massachusetts. John C. Calhoun was a prominent political thinker, a major power in Congress, and the secretary of war before becoming vice president. Four New Yorkers had already been vice president. Aaron Burr had been a U.S. senator and a minor Revolutionary War hero; George Clinton and Daniel Tompkins had been governors of New York and had held other important posts; and Martin Van Buren had been governor of New York, a U.S. senator, and secretary of state before being chosen as Andrew Jackson's running mate. Van Buren's vice president, Richard M. Johnson, had been a U.S. senator and was a hero of the War of 1812, credited with having personally killed the Indian leader Tecumseh at the Battle of the Thames in 1813. By comparison, Fillmore's career was fundamentally insignificant. He had never been elected to statewide office, had never served in the Senate, nor had he been in a presidential cabinet. Not surprisingly, at the Whig National Convention in Baltimore, Fillmore ran an increasingly distant third on the three ballots to choose Henry Clay's running mate. The nomination went to Theodore Frelinghuysen, the former senator from New Jersey who had gained the nickname the "Christian Statesman" for his six-hour speech denouncing Andrew Jackson's Indian removal policy. But as an avid colonizationist, his conservative views on slavery made him acceptable to southerners, and at the convention almost every southern delegate voted for him. Frelinghuysen's high moral standards made him the perfect northerner to balance with the somewhat sordid reputation of the slaveholding, dueling, hard-drinking Clay. The consolation prize for Fillmore was the nomination for governor of New York. It was not Fillmore's first choice, but it was certainly a step up from being a congressman from the remote western part of New York.

The Whigs assumed the presidential election would be something of a cakewalk, believing Clay would swamp Polk, a former Tennessee governor and Speaker of the House of Representatives. In 1840 the Whigs—with the Log Cabin and Hard Cider campaign of the war hero William Henry Harrison—had been an exciting party with an exciting ticket. Running as Tippecanoe and Tyler Too, they won nineteen states and defeated the incumbent Van Buren by more than 170 electoral votes and about 150,000 popular votes. The Whigs entered the campaign of 1844 with high expectations.

But the Whigs of 1844 were a different team. Clay and Frelinghuysen, with the less-than-snappy slogan Hurray, Hurray the
Country's Risin'; Vote for Clay and Frelinghuysen, seemed too conservative, too upper class, and too prim and proper (despite Clay's
"character" issues). The Whigs wanted to talk about the tariff and
currency, which were no longer exciting issues. Meanwhile, they
were whipsawed by Texas annexation (on which Clay waffled),
Manifest Destiny and the Oregon question (where Polk was
shrewdly aggressive and Clay was inconsistent and indecisive),
nativism (which pushed most new immigrant voters into the
Democratic Party), and the antislavery Liberty Party, which won
more than 62,000 votes nationally. The 1844 election turned out
to be a deep disappointment for the Whigs. Clay carried only
eleven states to Polk's fifteen, but the popular vote was razor thin,
as fewer than 39,000 votes separated the two candidates. Clay lost
New York by 5,100 votes—1 percent of the total cast. If he had
won New York, Clay would have had a majority of the electoral
votes and been elected president. Fillmore surely wondered if he
might have made the difference in carrying his home state.

Most frustrating of all for Fillmore and the Whigs, more than
15,000 New Yorkers voted for the antislavery Liberty Party. Had
the Liberty voters supported Clay, he would have won New York
and the election. Whigs like Fillmore believed that this vote should
have been theirs, and many historians have reiterated this, arguing
that the antislavery men should have supported the moderate Clay.
Such arguments are based on the assumption that for an antislavery voter Clay was the lesser of two evils. But such theories deeply
misunderstand the Liberty men. Clay, like Polk, was a slaveholder,
so he was unacceptable to these serious antislavery voters. The Liberty Party ran James G. Birney, a former slaveholder and ex-
colonizationist, who had long since denounced the ACS as racist
and fundamentally pro-slavery. The ACS wanted to remove free
blacks from the nation, which would actually strengthen slavery by
sending away those blacks whose very successes proved that slavery
could be abolished. For those truly opposed to slavery, there was no

significant difference between Master Clay of Kentucky and Master Polk of Tennessee. Despite Fillmore's belief that the Liberty men *should* have supported the Whigs, there was no reason for any of them to have voted for Clay.

Fillmore's race for the New York governorship was even less successful than Clay's campaign; he lost by 10,000 votes, winning only 231,057 to Silas Wright's 241,090. He believed that he would run better than Clay among opponents of slavery, but this did not happen. The Liberty candidate for governor in New York won 15,136 votes, about the same number as voted for Birney in the presidential race. Fillmore surely believed these Liberty men *should* have voted for him, because he was personally opposed to slavery. But nothing in Fillmore's campaign made him attractive to antislavery voters. He tried to avoid slavery by talking about the tariff, a key issue in national Whig politics, but one that generated little excitement. While campaigning, Fillmore opposed Texas annexation, but he refused to take a strong antislavery stand on the issue. Rather, he opposed annexation because he believed it was unconstitutional, would be costly, and would lead to a war with Mexico. But he did not oppose annexation on antislavery grounds, even though in running for a state office he did not have to worry about offending southerners. Had he opposed Texas annexation because it would create a new slave state and endorsed the kind of antislavery stands Governor Seward had taken, he might have won some Liberty votes. He might even have won over a few Democrats who opposed annexation on antislavery grounds. But he did not do this.

His defeat was also caused by his flirtations with nativists, his opposition to Catholic interests, and his generally anti-immigrant views. In his congressional races, Fillmore had successfully courted German Americans, and in 1843 he helped fund a German-language newspaper in Buffalo to shore up his political support. Many Germans were Protestants, and even those who were Catholic did not feel particularly discriminated against. But in his gubernatorial campaign Fillmore paid little attention to the Irish Catholic population in New York City and the smaller number of Irish voters upstate.

Instead, he openly courted the nativists, who were virulently anti-Catholic and anti-immigrant. During the gubernatorial campaign Fillmore prepared a letter to the anti-Catholic, anti-immigrant American Republican Party, indicating his support for mandatory Protestant Bible reading in the public schools. Fillmore gave the letter to the Whig editor Horace Greeley, who refused to deliver it to the nativists, correctly understanding that such a letter could harm Fillmore and the Whig Party.[18] But even without the publication of this letter (which confirms his views), Fillmore's hostility to immigrants and Catholics was transparent. The hostility cost him dearly, even in Buffalo, where he nearly lost his own ward because of immigrant voters.[19]

Following his defeat, Fillmore returned to his Buffalo law practice, blaming his loss mostly on "foreign Catholics."[20] He never acknowledged that his own flirtations with nativism cost him Catholic votes and that he lost the governorship because of his parochialism and bigotry. He also blamed the abolitionists for the Whig losses, but again he never considered that he lost the antislavery vote because he did not oppose Texas annexation on antislavery grounds, he refused to attack slavery in general, and he failed to suggest new programs and laws to create greater racial equality in the state. In other words, he blamed the Catholics (whom he had attacked) and the abolitionists (whom he would not support) for failing to vote for him.

In Buffalo he practiced law, gave interviews on politics, and took his place as a civic leader. The annexation of Texas, completed in December 1845, quickly led to war with Mexico in May 1846. Fillmore publicly argued that the war was in part to add slave territory to the nation, and he complained that southerners controlled Congress and the White House, even though the majority of the population lived in the North.[21] This was as close as he would ever come to publicly acknowledging and condemning what other northerners were beginning to see as the slave power conspiracy.

After his gubernatorial defeat, Fillmore was actively engaged in politics but not as a candidate. In 1846 he helped his law partner

Solomon Haven become mayor of Buffalo, and he helped his long-time friend and former law partner, Nathan K. Hall, win Fillmore's old seat in Congress. Fillmore could easily have had the Whig nomination for governor that year, but he did not want to run for governor again. What Fillmore did want was to ensure that his candidate, John Young, got the nomination rather than having it go to Thurlow Weed's candidate, Ira Harris. To accomplish this, Fillmore agreed to be a candidate, and on the first ballot at the Whig Convention he had the most votes. Indeed, his strategy almost backfired when he came within one vote of getting the nomination on the first ballot. Fortunately for Fillmore, because he did not actually want the nomination, his own campaign manager did not vote for him. Fillmore's floor managers then withdrew his name from consideration, and two ballots later Fillmore's candidate, John Young, won the nomination. Fillmore had successfully outmaneuvered the Seward-Weed faction of the party, and in November Young carried the state. The 1846 victory put the Whigs back in the governor's mansion, but it did not give them full control of the state. A new constitution provided for direct election for a number of top state offices, to be filled in 1847. Fillmore accepted the Whig nomination as state comptroller. Campaigning hard, with a united party behind him, he won by a margin of 38,000. This was a huge victory—indeed it would be the greatest victory of any Whig in the state's history. Symbolically, Fillmore sold his law books, closed his law office in Buffalo, and moved to Albany.

Given his strong interest in economics and finance, the comptrollership was the perfect position for him. Had he stayed there, he might have become a lasting figure in the state and a powerful political leader. However, his competence in running the office and his growing power in the state worked against a long tenure in Albany. Fillmore still had his eye on national politics, and the Weed-Seward faction in the state considered him to be an intolerable rival. Thus, Fillmore's ambition, and the ambitions of his Whig rivals, would push him onto the national stage a year later.

2

Texas, Mexico, and the Vice Presidency

James K. Polk's victory over Henry Clay in 1844 was directly tied to the Texas question. Ironically, by the time Polk actually took office, the lame-duck president, John Tyler, had mooted this issue by getting Congress to support a joint resolution allowing annexation of the independent republic.

When the 1844 campaign began, Henry Clay was unalterably opposed to annexation. Then he backed off, never quite clearly explaining where he stood. It cost him votes in the South and the West, where support for annexation was strong. He lost Georgia by 2,000 votes, while in 1840 Harrison had carried the state by more than 8,000 votes. Clay lost Louisiana by 699 votes, which Harrison had carried by almost 3,700 votes. And he lost Indiana (where support for expansion was strong) by 2,300 votes, while Harrison had carried it by more than 13,000 votes. A stronger position in favor of annexation—or even a more consistently clear position—might have changed the outcome in these states. Clay's equivocation may have hurt him among opponents of annexation as well. He lost Pennsylvania by just over 6,000 votes out of the more than 330,000 cast. A strong and principled stand against expansion and annexation might have attracted enough votes in that state to make the difference.

The returns in New York were even more dramatic in Clay's

defeat. Polk won 237,000 votes in that state to Clay's 232,000. Some 15,000 votes went to the Liberty Party. Had Clay strongly opposed expansion, it is not impossible that he would have won over some of those Liberty voters. But even without the Liberty voters, he still might have won the state if he had taken a clear position on annexation. In the governor's race, Fillmore's loss, and his equivocations on Texas, underscore the complexity of the election. Some 3,000 voters cast ballots in the gubernatorial race but not in the presidential race. Those votes went to Fillmore's Democratic opponent, Silas Wright. How could this be? The most logical answer is these were moderately antislavery Democrats. They could not support Polk because of his strong stand in favor of annexation, but they did not support Clay because he was so equivocal on the issue. Had Fillmore and Clay taken a firm and clear position on annexation, the outcome might have been different.

If a voter strongly supported annexation and expansion, then Polk was clearly his candidate. Polk's campaign slogan, "Fifty-Four Forty or Fight," indicated his willingness to challenge Great Britain to extend the nation's northwestern boundary into what is today British Columbia. This was a superb strategy, because while Polk was much more interested in Texas, asserting expansive claims in the Pacific Northwest made him palatable to many northerners. True, he wanted to annex Texas for slavery, but northerners could take consolation in the fact that he also wanted to add vast amounts of land on the Pacific slope that were presumably ill-suited for slavery. Thus, the Democrats could campaign in the South on Texas annexation and in the North on expanding the Oregon boundary. If a voter, north or south, believed in Manifest Destiny, then Polk was the right candidate.

But if a voter strongly opposed expansion, or just Texas annexation, as some New Yorkers did, Clay was not necessarily the candidate to choose. Clay's indecisive strategy may have been the kind that worked in Congress, pulling votes from both sides to win a moderate victory, but in the general election it may have left enough voters confused or disgusted to cost him the election.

Texas had complicated American politics from the moment the American settlers there declared independence from Mexico in early 1836. For the next eight years, Texas would unsuccessfully seek statehood. President Andrew Jackson rejected pleas from his friend Sam Houston to annex Texas and in fact initially refused to even recognize Texas independence because he did not want it to be an issue in the 1836 election. Even after Jackson's protégé Martin Van Buren was safely elected president, Jackson refused to recognize Texas independence until March 1, 1837, just three days before he left office. On that day Jackson signed a resolution passed by Congress to that effect and appointed Alcée Louis La Branche to be the U.S. chargé d'affaires to Texas. The administration refused to consider annexation because it meant a war with Mexico. Jackson was never one to run from a fight, but he prudently saw no reason to start a war over annexation. Van Buren and his slavehold-ing secretary of state, John Forsyth of Georgia, similarly showed no interest in annexation. Nor did William Henry Harrison when he became president. All three understood that annexation was not worth a war with Mexico, nor was it worth the huge political con-troversy over slavery that it would create. John Tyler, who became president when Harrison died in April 1841, was an aggressively pro-slavery expansionist and happily would have immediately annexed Texas if he had had the political clout to accomplish this goal. But Tyler had come to office as a Whig, and the vast majority of his party, which controlled Congress, was unalterably opposed to annexation. This was certainly true of his secretary of state, Daniel Webster.[1]

By 1843 Webster was out of the cabinet, replaced by the fanati-cally pro-slavery Abel Upshur of Virginia, and Tyler began to explore annexation. When Upshur died, Tyler replaced him with the equally pro-slavery John C. Calhoun of South Carolina, who vigorously supported Texas annexation. Never truly a Whig, Tyler opposed almost every policy the party stood for. The knowledge that he would never gain the Whig presidential nomination liber-ated Tyler to move forward on annexation, and in 1843 he began secret negotiations with Texas. In April 1844 representatives of Texas and the United States signed a treaty that would have brought Texas into the Union, but there was no chance the Senate would ratify it. In the end only sixteen senators voted for annexation, while thirty-five opposed it. A treaty required a two-thirds majority for ratification, but Tyler's treaty had a two-thirds majority *against* ratification.

The presidential election changed the dynamics on Texas. With Polk about to enter the White House and the Democrats poised to control the Senate, Tyler abandoned his strict constructionist constitutional scruples, which dictated that annexation was possible only by treaty. He asked Congress for a joint resolution to annex Texas, which would require a simple majority in each house. The congressional resolution, which Tyler signed on March 1, 1845, just before he left office, required assent from Texas. This was quickly achieved, although it took place after Polk was in office. The Texas Congress accepted annexation in June 1845, a state convention endorsed it in July, and in October Texas voters approved annexation by a vote of 7,664 to 430.[2] The irony of the 1844 election is that by the time Polk took office the most important issue he faced—Texas annexation—had been accomplished. The new president had only to implement the process, not resolve the issue. By December 1845 annexation was complete: another slave state had been added to the Union, and war with Mexico was looming. For Clay and Fillmore, the irony was not a pleasant one. The issue that had hurt them so much at the polls was no longer relevant.

· · ·

The Whigs' most compelling argument against annexation had been its potential for starting a war, because Mexico had never recognized Texas independence. As long as Texas remained an independent republic, the Mexican government had no strong incentive to actively assert its claim of ownership. In the years since declaring independence, Texas had hardly prospered; its government was weak, its treasury was empty, and its debt was mounting every year. Mexico knew that eventually the Texas experiment in independent government would fail. By 1843 the government in Austin was negotiating with Great Britain to intercede with Mexico to recognize Texas independence. It is hard to imagine that the slaveholding republic would have actually consented to any significant British influence in Texas because Britain was deeply hostile to slavery and had abolished it everywhere in its empire. Moreover, given the huge distance from London to Austin, it would have been difficult for Britain to maintain a presence in Texas in the face of any Mexican military opposition. Furthermore, since Mexico did not recognize Texas independence, it was unwilling to negotiate with Britain on the issue.

However unrealistic, the negotiations with Britain served a purpose. Some in the United States extravagantly predicted a permanent British presence on America's southern border. This played into long-standing American hostility to Britain, exacerbated by the unresolved dispute over the boundary between Queen Victoria's Canadian provinces and the U.S. territories in the Pacific Northwest. Some southerners argued that Britain would end slavery in Texas and that this would lead to slaves fleeing to the Republic of Texas. These predications helped the lame-duck Tyler convince a lame-duck Congress to annex Texas.

Polk, an ardent expansionist, was thrilled to come into office with the Texas question already resolved. Before the annexation was complete, Polk sent General Zachary Taylor and 1,500 soldiers to Louisiana, where they camped just across the river from Texas. This "Army of Observation," as Polk called it, was "the largest concentration of regulars since the Revolution,"[3] and it was clearly designed to provoke or intimidate Mexico. In July, even though Texas was not yet officially part of the United States, Polk ordered Taylor's army not only into Texas but to the city of Corpus Christi, on the south bank of the Nueces River—territory that Polk claimed for the United States but which Mexico justly claimed had never been part of Texas. Indeed, since 1836 the United States had recognized the Nueces as the boundary between Texas and Mexico.

Other international agreements supported the Mexican position on this issue. Polk, however, claimed that Texas—and hence the United States—owned all the land south to the Rio Grande. He began to take steps to secure this claim through military force. By August 1845 Polk had doubled the size of the American army in Texas, and in January 1846, just after Texas had entered the Union, Polk brazenly ordered American soldiers to march to the Rio Grande itself.[4] This was sure to provoke a Mexican response.

Polk also turned his attentions to other parts of Mexico. Even as he was taking steps that were likely to lead to war, Polk negotiated with Mexico to settle the boundary dispute in favor of his extravagant Texas claims. But Polk also wanted—really demanded—that Mexico sell the United States the territory that would become New Mexico, Arizona, Utah, Nevada, and California. He offered Mexico $25 million for this land, but from the start he probably understood such a transaction was unlikely to occur. Few nations willingly sell their own land to a neighbor. By the end of January, these negotiations had collapsed. Meanwhile, even as he sent emissaries to Mexico to negotiate, Polk was sending troops to seize what he wanted. By April a considerable American force, under Taylor's command, was camped on the northern bank of the Rio Grande in what had always been the Mexican state of Tamaulipas. On April 25 Mexican troops clashed with American soldiers on the northern side of the Rio Grande.

Polk's cabinet voted to seek a declaration of war from Congress on Friday, May 8. Polk planned to ask Congress for a declaration of war on Monday. General Taylor's communiqué about this battle reached Polk on Saturday, which simply made the president's war plans easier. On Monday, May 11, Polk sent his war message to Congress, detailing the breakdown of relations with Mexico, self-servingly blaming all of the conflict on the Mexicans, and asserting that "after a long series of menaces" the Mexican government had "at last invaded our territory and shed the blood of our fellow-citizens on our own soil." He asserted that "the grievous wrongs perpetrated by Mexico upon our citizens throughout a long period of years remain unredressed, and solemn treaties pledging her public faith for this redress have been disregarded." He noted that there was almost no trade with Mexico and that diplomatic contact had all but ceased. According to Polk, Mexico had rejected all American attempts at negotiation, and "now, after reiterated menaces, Mexico has passed the boundary of the United States, has invaded our territory and shed American blood upon the American soil. She has proclaimed that hostilities have commenced, and that the two nations are now at war." Polk's message conveniently ignored his provocative use of the military, his aggressive demands that Mexico sell a substantial portion of its country to the United States, and the fact that the fighting had taken place on disputed land. Instead, the president told Congress that "notwithstanding all our efforts to avoid it, [war] exists by the act of Mexico herself, [and] we are called upon by every consideration of duty and patriotism to vindicate with decision [sic] the honor, the rights, and the interests of our country."[5] Two days later, on Wednesday, May 13, the overwhelmingly Democratic Congress declared war.

The American war effort was remarkably successful given the huge distances the troops had to travel just to reach a combat zone, the difficult terrain, and the enormous health issues that plagued the army. The national army was minuscule at this time, and much of the war was fought by volunteers and militia men. Some 1,500 men died in combat, but another 11,000 died from other causes, mostly disease. Among the militiamen who never returned home were Henry Clay Jr., whose father had opposed Texas annexation and the war, and Archibald Yell, the former governor of Arkansas. Numerous future Civil War generals and leaders—including Ulysses S. Grant, William Tecumseh Sherman, George Meade, George McClellan, Robert E. Lee, Stonewall Jackson, James Longstreet, and future Confederate president Jefferson Davis—fought in the war as either regular officers or volunteers.[6]

Almost immediately after the war began, Colonel Stephen W. Kearney marched from Kansas to New Mexico (which included present-day Arizona). Reaching Santa Fe in August 1846, he claimed the entire region for the United States. Kearney then led 300 men to California, where he captured San Diego. In January 1847 Kearney marched north, joined with naval forces under Commodore Robert Stockton, and defeated Mexican forces in the Battle of Los Angeles. Meanwhile, in June 1846 American settlers in northern California joined a small force, led by John C. Frémont, which seized Sacramento and briefly created the California Republic (better known, because of its flag, as the Bear Flag Republic). In January 1847 Frémont signed the Treaty of Cahuenga, under which the Mexican forces surrendered California to the Americans, and on March 1 Kearney formally established a provisional American government there. The Americans had now secured all the land that Polk had offered to buy from Mexico the previous year.

In Mexico itself, military success took longer and was more costly. But under the command of Generals Zachary Taylor and Winfield Scott, American forces pushed deep into Mexico. In February, at Buena Vista, Taylor defeated a much larger force under the command of Mexico's president, General Antonio López de Santa Anna. Meanwhile, the U.S. Navy successfully blockaded Veracruz, which General Scott captured in March 1847. In April, even before he had news of these victories, Polk had sent Nicholas Trist to negotiate a peace treaty. In August, Trist negotiated a cease-fire and began peace talks with Mexican commissioners. At this point General Scott's army was less than ten miles from Mexico City, and the Mexicans clearly lacked the ability to stop the American forces. On September 7, 1847, the Mexicans broke off negotiations; a week later Scott's forces captured Mexico City. Shortly after, Santa Anna resigned and fled the country. The United States had attained a complete military victory but was unable to end the war because there was no government in place in Mexico to surrender or make peace.

Further complicating this situation, Polk had recalled Trist, effectively denying him any official power to negotiate with the Mexicans. Trist ignored the recall and, acting as a private citizen, resumed negotiations with Mexican commissioners after Santa

Anna left the country. On February 2, 1848, Trist signed the Treaty of Guadalupe Hidalgo, which gave the United States everything it had tried to buy before the war, while the United States agreed to pay $15 million directly to the Mexican government and provide another $3 million to settle American claims against Mexico. When the treaty reached Washington in February, Polk was furious. Even though he had recalled Trist, he was now saddled with a treaty that gave him everything he initially had hoped to acquire. By this time Polk was contemplating taking even more Mexican territory, and now he could not continue the war, given the favorable treaty Trist had sent him. Thus, the Senate received a treaty the president did not really want, to end a war the president actually wanted to continue, negotiated and signed by an American envoy who had technically been fired by the president. Nevertheless, on March 10, 1848, the Senate ratified the treaty, and all of the negotiations and exchanges of signed documents were completed by the end of May.

The United States was once again at peace, but it was now about 555,000 square miles larger than it had been before the war. The Mexican Cession included all of the present-day states of California, Nevada, and Utah, almost all of present-day Arizona (the United States would secure the rest with the Gadsden Purchase in 1853), and parts of New Mexico, Colorado, and Wyoming. In addition, the treaty confirmed the Rio Grande as the southern boundary of Texas.

. . .

Most Whigs had opposed Texas annexation because it would lead to a war with Mexico. When it did, they opposed the war as an unnecessary conflict started by an overly belligerent, warmongering president. Like the Democrats, the Whigs believed in America's destiny, but their notion of greatness did not center on territorial expansion, especially if it could only be achieved by aggressive war. Whigs believed that internal development and economic growth would be far better for the nation than going to war over the vast stretches of desert that constituted Texas, New Mexico, and what was then known as Upper California. The tariff of 1842, which Fillmore had guided through Congress, as well as Fillmore's persistent advocacy of a federal program for river and harbor improvements, especially on the Great Lakes, reflected traditional Whig notions of American progress that would lead to greatness. Economic development, not conquest, was how Whigs would lead America to her manifest destiny.

Slavery played into this Whig opposition in two ways. Many northern Whigs considered the war part of a larger pro-slavery scheme to grab more land to spread human bondage across the continent. Southern Whigs were not necessarily opposed to more land for slavery and surely did not endorse the idea that the war was a pro-slavery adventure. But southern Whigs believed the war was unnecessary, especially after the acquisition of Texas. They were especially worried that the war would unsettle the status quo on slavery and reopen the debate over slavery in the territories. Even some Democrats, like the ardently pro-slavery southern nationalist John C. Calhoun, feared the war would stimulate antislavery agitation that could only hurt the South.

While the war was being fought, Millard Fillmore remained essentially a bystander, without an elective office. In addition to his law practice, he was the chancellor of the newly created University of Buffalo, which gave him honor and prestige but further removed him from politics. Fillmore was still a leader of the New York Whigs though, and as a private citizen he weighed in against the war. He argued that "the interests of the North" were being "sacrificed" by Polk and the Democrats in a "wild and wicked scheme of foreign conquest" in order to add "another slave territory to the United States."[7] This was as close as he would ever come to acknowledging the pernicious affects of slavery on the nation. But even as he attacked Polk's foreign policy, Fillmore complained of Polk's veto of a rivers and harbors bill that would have dramatically improved trade and commerce on the Great Lakes and been especially beneficial to Buffalo, sitting as it was on Lake Erie and at the terminus of the Erie Canal.[8] A war to gain new lands for slavery bothered Fillmore but not nearly as much as Polk's veto of the bill for public improvements or his dismantling of the tariff Fillmore had guided through the House of Representatives.

The Whigs were not the only politicians troubled by the connection between slavery and the war. Northern Democrats were eager proponents of manifest destiny and territorial expansion, but they were sensitive to the criticism that the war was part of a larger pro-slavery conspiracy. Opposition to slavery was growing in the North, and pro-war Democrats there feared that in the next election they would be defeated by a coalition of Whigs, Liberty Party voters, and antislavery Democrats for spreading slavery into the West. The issue came to a head at the end of the congressional session in August 1846. Polk had asked for $2 million to finance peace negotiations with Mexico and facilitate the acquisition of Mexican territory. Congressman David Wilmot of Pennsylvania, a first-term Democrat who had previously been completely loyal to Polk, proposed a rider to the appropriations bill—the Wilmot Proviso—declaring that "as an express and fundamental condition to the acquisition of any territory from the Republic of Mexico by the United States, by virtue of any treaty which may be negotiated between them, and to the use by the Executive of the moneys herein appropriated, neither slavery nor involuntary servitude shall ever exist in any part of said territory, except for crime, whereof the party shall first be duly convicted." By a vote of 80 to 64 the Wilmot Proviso passed the House. The divisions were sectional and bipartisan, as northern Whigs and Democrats joined forces to stop the spread of slavery into the West, while all but three southerners voted against it.[9]

The appropriations bill died in August 1846, when the session came to an end before the Senate could vote on the bill. Over the next four years, various versions of the Wilmot Proviso would be introduced. Northerners dominated the House of Representatives (where seats were allocated on the basis of population), and with almost unanimous northern support—from Whigs and Democrats— the proviso easily passed in that body. In the Senate, southerners were consistently able to stop the proviso. From the end of 1846 until May 1848, there were fifteen slave states and only fourteen free states. Southern senators could easily block the proviso, but they lacked the power to pass any legislation without northern support in the House. Wisconsin statehood in 1848 gave northerners parity in the Senate, but southerners could always find a few doughfaces—northern men with southern principles—to vote with them to kill the proviso.[10] During this period, both houses of Congress eventually passed the necessary appropriations to continue the war and secure the peace, but Congress could accomplish little more. With the war over, Congress had to come to terms with the problem of slavery in the territories.

This problem was hardly a new issue. In 1784 the Congress, operating under the Articles of Confederation, considered Thomas Jefferson's "Plan of Government for the Western Territory," which would have banned slavery in all of the western territories, after the year 1800. However, by 1784 thousands of slaves were already living in what would become Kentucky and Tennessee, and more were arriving every day. There were also about a thousand slaves in what would later become Indiana and Illinois. As the historian William M. Wiecek has noted, Jefferson's ordinance "was, in effect, a permission to the western territories and states to establish slavery and retain it to 1800." By then there would have been so many slaves in the region, and so much political power vested in the region's master class, that it would have been almost impossible not to repeal or modify the ban. Whatever the ban might have accomplished, Congress rejected Jefferson's proposal. This was Jefferson's last attempt to limit the spread of slavery, but it was an opening salvo in an eighty-year struggle over slavery in the western territories.[11]

Three years later, in 1787, while the Constitutional Convention met in Philadelphia, the Confederation Congress passed the Northwest Ordinance, which banned slavery north and west of the Ohio River. The ordinance did not immediately end slavery in the Northwest Territory, and some blacks would be held in bondage in Illinois

into the 1840s.[12] But the ordinance did establish two principles:
first, that Congress had the power, and perhaps even the duty, to
regulate slavery in the national territories and, second, that slavery
should never expand north of the Ohio River. Since at the time the
United States terminated at the Mississippi River, the ordinance
appeared to have permanently settled the issue of slavery in the
territories. But the acquisition of the Louisiana Territory in 1803
undermined the ordinance and reopened the issue of slavery in the
territories, as most of the Louisiana Territory was north of the
southern terminus of the Ohio River. In 1803 no one considered
whether the Northwest Ordinance applied to the new territory or
whether the ordinance was applicable only to the territories owned
in 1787.

The question of slavery in the new territories did not arise until
Missouri, almost entirely north of the southern terminus of the
Ohio River, sought admission to the Union in 1819. At the time of
the Louisiana Purchase, residents there owned a substantial number
of slaves and more moved in afterward. In 1803, when he accomplished the purchase, President Jefferson no longer favored con-
taining slavery and did nothing to stop its spread west. Nor did his
close ally and successor, James Madison, see any reason to attempt
to restrict the spread of slavery in the new territory. In 1810 the
first census after the acquisition of Louisiana showed that the Missouri Territory had only 2,875 slaves, but by 1820 the slave population had grown to more than 10,200. In 1819 Missouri sought
admission to the Union as a slave state, which led to a protracted
debate over the status of slavery in the territories.

The result of this debate was the Missouri Compromise, passed
in 1820. The compromise admitted Missouri as a slave state and
allowed Maine to break off from Massachusetts and enter the
Union as a free state. This kept the balance of slave and free states
even, with twelve of each. The most important provision of the
compromise concerned the status of slavery in the remaining territories. Under the compromise, slavery would be permanently
banned north and west of the southern boundary of Missouri—the

36°30′ parallel. The architect of this statute was Henry Clay, and his role as the "Great Compromiser" catapulted him to national prominence. It made him a presidential candidate in 1824 and led to his becoming John Quincy Adams's secretary of state in 1825. It secured his position as a Whig leader for the rest of his life.

By the time of the Mexican War, most northerners saw the Missouri Compromise as an almost sacred act, something close to a founding document like the Declaration of Independence or the Constitution itself. From 1820 until the mid-1840s, the compromise kept slavery from spreading into new places while allowing for new slave and free states to enter the Union. The compromise also placed a limit on slavery that northerners assumed would put it, in Abraham Lincoln's words, "in the course of ultimate extinction."[13] Under the Missouri Compromise, the only territory left open to slavery consisted of the future states of Arkansas, Oklahoma, and Florida. In 1820 Americans could look forward to a time when there would be no new slave states and an increasing number of free states. This promise was the trade-off Henry Clay used to gain a sufficient number of northern votes in the House of Representatives to bring Missouri into the Union as a slave state. Texas annexation added one more slave state to the Union but did not delay the end of the admission of new slave states, nor did it change the expectation that there would soon be an end to new slave states entering the Union.

The Mexican War, however, radically altered the calculus. About half the territory acquired from Mexico was south of the 36°30′ parallel. If the Missouri Compromise line governed the Mexican Cession, slavery could spread to present-day Arizona and New Mexico, southern California, and a small portion of Nevada. However, southern nationalists had long objected to the ban on slavery in the territories, arguing that it unconstitutionally deprived slave owners of the opportunity to settle the western territories. Now, southerners argued that they would not be satisfied with merely the southern portion of the Mexican Cession. They wanted access to all of the new lands. Many northerners, meanwhile, were not interested in extending the Missouri line either, because they wanted to stop the spread of slavery into these new territories. Thus, the Wilmot Proviso paralyzed Congress. The huge northern majority in the House would not allow organization of the territories without a ban on slavery, while in the Senate the southerners, with a few doughface allies, could block the proviso.

The first vote over the Wilmot Proviso, in August 1846, indicated that slavery had reemerged as the "nemesis of the Constitution"[14] and of the political process. For the first time since the Missouri debates, the House was divided not by party but by slavery and sectionalism. Historians critical of Wilmot and the abolitionists have long condemned this vote as an example of aggressive attacks on slavery by northerners. But the vote also shows that southerners were equally aggressive, demanding that slavery be allowed in the Southwest (where it had been banned under Mexican law) and in Utah and Nevada, which were north of the Missouri Compromise line. Most northerners had accepted Texas as a slave state because slavery was already entrenched there. Similarly, a number of northerners had been willing to admit Missouri as a slave state in part because slavery was already there. But there were no slaves in the lands that the United States was about to acquire from Mexico, so, from a northern perspective, this was the perfect moment to stop the western spread of human bondage.

Some people, including General Zachary Taylor, thought the proviso was unnecessary because slavery was not economically viable in the Southwest. Many historians have argued this point as well. However, virtually every southerner in Congress rejected this argument. Slave labor was cheaper than hiring free people, and as long as there was land to cultivate, southerners wanted to use their slaves. Moreover, many southerners believed California was well suited to slavery. Once gold was discovered, they were even more anxious to bring their slaves to the Pacific Coast. The gold rush began in northern California, far above the 36°30' parallel. Any application of the Missouri Compromise line would prevent southerners from using their slaves to mine gold. For both southerners and northerners, the Wilmot debate was not symbolic. It was a real debate over how the West would be settled. It was a debate over slavery or freedom, bondage or liberty, in the newly acquired western territories.

. . .

In the aftermath of the 1846 midterm elections, the Whigs believed they would recapture the White House in 1848. Polk had run on the promise of serving only one term, but there was deep dissatisfaction with him anyway, and the Democrats lacked any attractive candidates. Henry Clay still yearned for the nomination, but his time had passed, even though he could not admit it. Equally hungry for the nomination was Daniel Webster, but he, like Clay, had been seeking the office for too long. Both men were in their sixties, and in the 1840s that was old. Furthermore, both had been on the political scene since the War of 1812. They were "old news," with few new ideas but with liabilities that had been accumulating over the years. Perhaps their greatest liability, aside from their age and lack of freshness, was that both were such orthodox Whigs. In order to win, the Whigs needed a new face, someone who could rally the stalwarts, avoid antagonizing the North or the South, and bring new voters to the cause.[15]

An early favorite was Supreme Court justice John McLean of Ohio. He had served in the administrations of Monroe, John Quincy Adams, and Jackson and could legitimately tie himself to the founding of the nation. A respected jurist, he appeared to be above politics, in sharp contrast with lifelong politicians like Webster and Clay. In fact, McLean was as hungry for the presidency as Clay or Webster. John Quincy Adams noted that McLean "thinks of nothing but the Presidency by day and dreams of nothing else by night,"[16] but most Americans did not know that side of McLean, so his candidacy would have provided a distinguished but fresh face for the campaign. The advantage of being on the Court—that he was above the fray—was also a disadvantage because he could not openly campaign for the office, and he was constrained from making too many speeches and public appearances.

Slavery complicated McLean's candidacy as well. In *Prigg v. Pennsylvania* (1842) the Supreme Court had upheld the Fugitive Slave Act of 1793, which allowed masters to find their fugitive slaves, bring them before any court, state or federal, and, after getting a certificate of removal, take them home. Because of the act's lax evidentiary standards, most northern states had passed personal liberty laws that required higher standards of proof to remove an alleged fugitive slave from the state. In an 8 to 1 decision, Justice Joseph Story held that the 1793 law was fully constitutional and that state laws were unconstitutional if they interfered with the return of a fugitive slave. In striking down Pennsylvania's personal liberty law, Story severely limited the ability of the northern states to protect free blacks from kidnapping. But almost as an aside, Justice Story noted that the free states could not be compelled to enforce the federal law of 1793 and that they might even refuse to do so. This portion of the opinion deeply rankled the South and led to the demand for a new and tougher fugitive slave law. Despite relieving the states of an obligation to enforce the law, northerners and southerners alike saw this as the most pro-slavery decision ever issued by the Court.[17] McLean had been the sole dissenter in this case, because he believed that the state personal liberty laws were not only constitutional but essential to prevent kidnapping. This made him a problematic candidate in the South. Nevertheless, in 1846 he seemed to be the candidate to beat. The issue of slavery in the new territories had not yet emerged, and McLean's friends were certain they could sufficiently explain away his dissent in *Prigg* to make him viable in the South, because he had also decided other fugitive slave cases in favor of masters.

But McLean's candidacy, along with those of Clay and Webster, began to fade after Zachary Taylor's military successes. Early in the war, some Whigs had approached Taylor about the presidency, but he had adamantly refused to consider running. However, as Taylor's fame rose, Polk tried to undermine the general's effectiveness. This merely enhanced Taylor's credentials among the Whigs. Ironically, because Taylor was a successful general who had never been in favor of the war, he seemed to be the ideal candidate for the Whigs. Taylor, the Whigs hoped, would be attractive to those who supported the war, because he was a victorious general, as well as those Whigs who opposed the war, because he had become persona non grata with Polk. Support for Taylor increased dramatically after his stunning victory at Buena Vista in February 1847. There Taylor's army of 6,000 men defeated Santa Anna's 20,000 troops. The general himself showed enormous personal courage during the battle. In a futile attempt to undermine Taylor's popularity, President Polk stupidly complained that the battle was unnecessary. But this criticism only enhanced the growing stature of a successful general. By now, Taylor was thoroughly disgusted with Polk and was feuding with General Winfield Scott, whom Polk had placed above him in the chain of command. In March 1847 Taylor wrote to the Kentucky Whig politician John J. Crittenden that he still supported Henry Clay and did not want to run for office, but he added, "If my friends deem it for the good of country that I be a candidate . . . so be it."[18] In December seven Whig congressmen, known as the "Young Indians," organized a Taylor for President Club. Five were southerners, including Robert Toombs of Georgia and Alexander Stephens of Georgia, who in 1861 would become vice president of the Confederacy. One of the two northerners was Abraham Lincoln of Illinois, a lifelong admirer of Henry Clay who saw the war hero Taylor as the best candidate to carry the election. Significantly, Lincoln had opposed the war and had challenged the truth of Polk's claim that American soldiers had been killed on American soil. But he and other opponents of the Mexican War saw no contradiction in supporting the popular general. By the spring more than forty other Whig congressmen had joined the Young Indians.

Taylor's presidential credentials were curious. He had never formally joined a political party and had never even voted in an election. He was a Virginia native, raised on the Kentucky frontier, who owned plantations in Louisiana and Mississippi along with nearly 150 slaves. These credentials secured his credibility in the South, while his status as a brave war hero—even in a war Whigs opposed—made him viable in the North. He appeared to be a political novice and a nonpartisan man of the people. He also had a strong record of demanding fair treatment of Indians and enforcement of treaty rights, which resonated with Whigs, especially in the North, who had long been disgusted with the aggressive Indian removal policies of every administration since Andrew Jackson. Taylor had opposed Texas annexation, even as he heroically secured Texas and much of Mexico with his military skills and courage. Old Rough and Ready was unpretentious to the point that the commanding general was sometimes mistaken for a common soldier. Taylor was actually more politically savvy than people realized. His father had been a politician in Kentucky, and he was a cousin of James Madison. Moreover, no antebellum officer rose to the rank of major general without powerful political skills. As the historian Michael Holt has persuasively demonstrated, Taylor carefully positioned himself to be the "new Cincinnatus, a man who, like Washington, stood above party, a man without personal ambition dedicated to the common good, a man who indeed might be able to restore the glories of the early republic."[19] His was a self-conscious and shrewd strategy to gain the presidential nomination.

However, Taylor's candidacy concerned northern Whigs for three major reasons. First, he was not seen as a "true" Whig. While he had always been a supporter of Henry Clay and hated the Democrats, Taylor had no record on the key Whig issues, such as banking, the tariff, and internal improvements. Henry Clay, despite his many liabilities, was still the favorite. If there was a "Mr. Whig," Clay was that man.[20]

Many northerners were also concerned because Taylor was a slaveholding southerner. They feared he would not only alienate northern antislavery voters but also have a pro-slavery administration. This led to their third fear: that Taylor favored the spread of slavery into the territories. His true views, unknown to most people, were just the opposite. Mexican law had prohibited slavery in this area, and Taylor saw no reason to change this. Taylor also opposed the Wilmot Proviso, but only because he considered it unnecessary; no sane southerner, he believed, would bring his slaves to the deserts of New Mexico. As a cotton planter, he could not imagine any useful purpose for slaves in the arid Southwest, although he never openly articulated this position.

At the Whig Convention in May, southern support for Taylor was strong, while northern Whigs were deeply divided among five other candidates. Henry Clay's supporters were shocked when, on the first ballot, their man ran second with 97 votes to Taylor's 111. On the next two ballots, Clay lost 23 delegates, while Taylor gained 22. Taylor won the nomination on the next ballot.[21] Most of his support came from the slave states, where he had 106 of the 112 delegates, even though two other southerners, Clay and General Winfield Scott of Virginia, were also in the running. Moreover, most of his northern support came from the smaller states. He had only 20 of the 97 votes from New York, Massachusetts, Ohio, and Pennsylvania.[22] It took the Whig Convention only four ballots to nominate Taylor, while the great leaders of the party, Clay and Webster, saw their vote totals drop with each round of voting.

Taylor's nomination guaranteed that his running mate would be a northerner and a party regular. In nominating an aging general with uncertain political views, the Whigs were not going to make the same mistake they had in 1840. In that year the vice presidential candidate, John Tyler, was a states' rights, strict constructionist conservative who had fallen out with the Democratic Party over Jackson's strong presidency. He was an ideal running mate for Harrison because he was a slaveholding southerner, but Tyler had almost no interest in any Whig issues, other than hating Jackson. Harrison's death, just a month after his inauguration, had saddled the Whigs with a president they came to despise. The party was taking a similar chance nominating Taylor, but at least he was a lifelong supporter of the Whigs, far closer to the party's mainstream than Tyler had ever been. If Taylor ran with a strong Whig running mate, the party's future would be more secure. That running mate also had to be moderately opposed to slavery extension in order to balance Taylor's status as a planter and slave owner but not so antislavery as to offend southerners.

At the Whig Convention fourteen men were put forward for the vice presidential nomination, but only four were serious contenders: Abbot Lawrence of Massachusetts, Thomas Ewing of Ohio, and two New Yorkers, William H. Seward and Millard Fillmore.

Lawrence was a millionaire textile manufacturer and industrialist who was willing and able to spend a significant amount of his own money on the campaign. He had been a two-term congressman, a leader of the Massachusetts Whigs, and a diplomat who had helped negotiate the Webster-Ashburton Treaty with Great Britain in 1842. He was sophisticated, worldly, and enormously wealthy. He was a leader of the conservative "Cotton Whigs" of the party, the wing Charles Sumner would label the "Lords of the Loom," who were aligned with the southern "Lords of the Lash."[23] Lawrence had opposed Texas annexation but was unacceptable to the antislavery Conscience Whigs because of his close ties to the South. His nomination would have further alienated the antislavery wing of the party, already smarting from Taylor's nomination, and that surely weakened his position. Under the assumption that Taylor would be inflexibly pro-slavery, the Conscience Whigs demanded someone safer on these issues. Lawrence might have overcome these liabilities, but he could not overcome local Massachusetts politics. In 1844 he had been a leading supporter of Henry Clay, for which Daniel Webster, who had wanted the nomination, never forgave him. At the 1848 convention, Webster's son made it clear that Lawrence was unacceptable to the most important Whig politician in Massachusetts, and that was enough to seal his fate. Intrigue among the Massachusetts Whigs doomed Lawrence.[24]

A similar intrigue among the Ohio Whigs likewise doomed Thomas Ewing, a former U.S. senator who had served under Harrison and Tyler as secretary of the Treasury and who was surely the most qualified of the potential vice presidential candidates. Ewing was acceptable to the Conscience Whigs and the Cotton Whigs and would have helped bring the huge state of Ohio into the Whig column. But just before balloting for the vice presidential nomination, an Ohio delegate asserted that Ewing wanted his name withdrawn. This ruse was an act of vengeance perpetrated by one of Ewing's home-state rivals, but no one challenged the claim and Ewing's name was withdrawn. Twenty years later "Ewing was still fuming" that he had lost a possible chance to be president.[25]

The other two potential vice presidential candidates were the New York rivals Seward and Fillmore. Seward probably had no real interest in the job—he was far too energetic and forceful to be happy in such a role. Some months earlier he had considered publicly announcing his lack of interest in the nomination but then backed away from so precipitous a move. Fillmore's allies in the New York party had been scheming for more than a year to secure the vice presidential nomination, and Seward feared that as vice president Fillmore would become the most powerful player in the New York party. Seward truly believed this would be a disaster.

Part of Seward's opposition to Fillmore was narrowly partisan: if Fillmore controlled the New York Whigs, Seward and his close ally Thurlow Weed would no longer have any influence in party patronage. But Seward's opposition was also substantive. Seward differed from Fillmore on race, slavery, immigration, and Catholicism. Seward was a firm supporter of black rights and hostile to slavery. As governor, he had prevented the extradition of free blacks to Virginia and signed the law immediately freeing any slaves brought into the state. By this time Seward was also famous for his argument before the U.S. Supreme Court in *Jones v. Van Zandt* (1847), in which he had represented an abolitionist who was sued for helping fugitive slaves escape. Seward lost the case, and the abolitionist John Van Zandt was virtually bankrupted, but in arguing the case Seward had secured his reputation as a friend of liberty and an opponent of human bondage. Seward's nomination would thus offend the southern wing of the party, just as Lawrence was unacceptable to the antislavery wing. In New York Seward had firmly opposed anti-Catholic policies, which made him suspect among the nativists in the party and those Whig leaders who hoped to court the anti-Catholic vote, especially in Pennsylvania, the state with the second largest number of electoral votes. In addition, many Whigs disliked the ambitious and sometimes arrogant Seward and distrusted his close ally Weed. If a non–New Yorker (such as Lawrence) was on the ticket, then it would be likely that a victorious Taylor would make a New Yorker—probably Seward—secretary of state. Seward did not in fact want to be vice president, which had been a political death sentence for almost every man who held the job. Seward actually wanted the vice presidency to go to Lawrence or someone else who was not from New York. That was Weed's plan as well. Thus, at the last minute Seward's allies withdrew his name from consideration, in the hope that the nomination would go to Lawrence and set up Seward to be secretary of state.

At the convention, Fillmore's allies aggressively argued that Lawrence would alienate too many in the North. John A. Collier, a leader of the anti-Seward wing of the party who hoped to be the new U.S. senator from New York, nominated Fillmore and lobbied a number of state delegations, telling southerners that Fillmore was safe on slavery while disingenuously telling northerners that Fillmore supported the Wilmot Proviso (although in fact he did not). Collier's lobbying worked in part because, unlike Taylor, Fillmore was a real Whig and committed to Whig policies on economics, tariffs, and banking. He had avoided debates over racial equality in New York and was not actively antislavery, so he would not threaten the South. Indeed, the fact that he was Seward's rival made him more acceptable to southern Whigs. On the other hand, he was not openly a Cotton Whig, and since he had never said much about slavery in the territories, he seemed acceptable to the antislavery wing of the party. Collier urged northern delegates to support Fillmore, claiming he was clearly better than Lawrence on the slavery issue (although he was not). He was openly hostile to Catholics and would satisfy the nativists. And, as a New Yorker, he was the perfect foil for the Seward-Weed wing of the party.

The Whig ticket required a less controversial northerner than

Lawrence or Seward on the second spot, and Fillmore fit the bill. Fillmore also came from New York, where he had just won a stunning victory for comptroller of the state. Clay had lost New York by about 5,000 votes. A proven New York vote getter, such as Fillmore, could bring that state into the Whig column. On the first ballot, Fillmore had 115 votes to Lawrence's 109 with 51 votes scattered among other candidates. Had Seward and Weed been more active and a bit more prepared, they might have brought those votes to Lawrence and given him the nomination. Instead, Fillmore's supporters acted quickly and decisively, and on the second ballot Fillmore had the nomination with 173 votes to Lawrence's 87.[26]

Thus, Fillmore found himself in the second spot on the national ticket. It surely must have surprised him, even though he had fought hard for the nomination. He had little national political experience. Except for his four terms in Congress, he had barely lived or even traveled outside of central and western New York. Ultimately, Fillmore's utter lack of qualifications mattered little. Candidates did not directly campaign in 1848, and thus Fillmore did not have to make speeches, travel the nation, or expose himself to the media. If he won, he would have a prestigious, ceremonial office with little power. The only job the vice president had was to preside over the Senate and vote to break ties. Except for the accidental presidency of Tyler, no vice president had ever had to step into the presidency without being elected. The vice presidency was mostly honorific and a one-way ticket to political obscurity. In fact, since Thomas Jefferson's election, only one vice president—Martin Van Buren—had been nominated by his party to run for president.[27] But for Millard Fillmore, the parvenu from Sempronius, New York, this was a huge moment.

3

A Heartbeat Away

Between the elections of 1844 and 1848, the United States had settled the border dispute with Britain in the Pacific Northwest, annexed Texas, added four new states, won a war with Mexico, and vastly increased its physical size. All this success had brought nothing but misery to its political leaders. Congress was paralyzed over the Wilmot Proviso and the status of slavery in the new territories. The presidential election of 1848 brought this discontent into sharp focus.

The Democrats had pushed for the war with Mexico, and the enormous success of that conflict tore the party apart. Their nominee for president, Lewis Cass, had little to recommend him other than that he was a northerner acceptable to southern Democrats. However, a substantial number of northern Democrats could not accept his seemingly pro-slavery position on the territories, while others could not forgive him for his role in denying the party's nomination in 1844 to former president Martin Van Buren and then beating out Van Buren for the 1848 nomination as well. Thus, in 1848, Van Buren ran for president on the ticket of the newly formed Free Soil Party, which brought together antislavery Democrats, Conscience Whigs, and Liberty Party men. This was not a true antislavery party because the Free Soilers focused only on stopping the spread of slavery into the West, but it was the first time any significant party, with a nationally famous candidate, challenged slavery.[1]

The Whigs had opposed the Mexican War and then nominated General Zachary Taylor, a hero of that war, who also owned about 150 slaves on his Louisiana plantations. Southern Whigs were delighted because they assumed that Taylor would support the spread of slavery into the West. As the historian David Potter has noted, they "regarded Taylor as their man, [and] trusting him as a southerner, they had not even asked him to state his position on the territories."[2] To even ask the question of a fellow slaveholding planter would be unseemly. Northern Whigs, who opposed the spread of slavery into the territories, could hardly stand the idea of the slaveholding Taylor as their candidate. They insisted on at least securing one of their own for the vice presidential nominee, whose tiebreaking vote in the Senate might be crucial in banning slavery in the Mexican Cession. They counted on Millard Fillmore to assume that role. Yet just as no southerners asked Taylor about his views on slavery and the territories, no one bothered to ask Fillmore where he stood on these issues. Northerners mistakenly believed that the former congressman from Buffalo *must* be an opponent of slavery.

As Potter observed, "only gradually did" the southern Whigs "learn that they had played an incredible trick on themselves" by counting on Taylor to support their position on slavery in the territories.[3] Similarly, only gradually did the northerners discover that they too had played an "incredible trick on themselves." While the southern slaveholding Taylor opposed the spread of slavery into the territories, the northerner Fillmore had no strong feelings on the issue and would ultimately sign legislation to allow slavery in the new territories.

In the three-way contest, the Whigs did well, although the outcome was hardly decisive. Taylor and Fillmore captured a majority of both northern and southern electoral votes. They won seven of the ten largest states, including the two largest in the North and the two largest in the South. They carried eight slave states and seven free states and won 1,360,000 popular votes, to Cass's 1,220,000 and Van Buren's 291,000.

Whether Van Buren shifted the election to Taylor is unclear. In New York, Van Buren's 120,000 votes came mostly from Democrats, but in Ohio it is likely that antislavery Whigs, unable to stomach another slaveholding president after Tyler and Polk, voted for the Free Soil ticket, putting that state in the Democratic column. What should have been central to Fillmore—and what matters to historians today—is not the way Van Buren may have shifted electoral votes, but the overall power of his campaign. Running in only fifteen northern states, Van Buren won more than 290,000 votes. In four states he won more than 25 percent of the popular vote, and in three of them—Massachusetts, Vermont, and New York—he won more votes than the Democrat, Lewis Cass. In ten of the fifteen northern states, Van Buren's total was enough to have changed the outcome if his voters had supported the losing candidate. The Free Soil vote demonstrated how powerful northern sentiment was against slavery. It was a lesson Millard Fillmore failed to learn.

The Free Soil Party also affected state elections. Free Soilers in Ohio held the balance of power. They first offered to vote with the Whigs, which would have given them control of the state legislature, in return for sending the antislavery Whig Joshua Giddings to the Senate.[4] Most of Ohio's Whigs despised Giddings because of his radical antislavery views; they refused the offer to control the legislature and also lost the opportunity to elect a Whig (even a radical antislavery Whig) to the U.S. Senate. The Free Soilers then turned to the Democrats, who were notoriously hostile to black rights and generally pro-slavery. But the Democrats agreed to send the equally antislavery Salmon P. Chase to the Senate and to repeal Ohio's racially oppressive Black Laws in return for Free Soil support in giving the Democrats control of the state legislature.[5] Slavery had clearly changed the nature of politics in that key state. Had Millard Fillmore been an astute politician, he might have observed these trends and taken note that northern discomfort over slavery was a new political fact to be reckoned with. His failure to understand this dramatically undermined his presidency and his subsequent political career.

Unlike modern elections, antebellum presidential candidates rarely chose their own running mates.[6] In fact, Taylor had never met Fillmore when the two were nominated. As noted in chapter 2, the Whig Convention considered a number of candidates, and political rivalries and local politics, as much as the needs of the national ticket, led the party to Fillmore, the least prominent of the candidates. Thus, despite his relative obscurity, or maybe because of it, he emerged as the vice presidential candidate.

Fillmore had remained mostly in Albany from his nomination to the election, and, like other candidates for national office in this period, he made no speeches. The campaign was conducted via surrogates, rallies, editorials, and letters. In the South, the Democrats accused Fillmore of being an abolitionist. Fillmore responded to these accusations with letters vehemently denying the charges. He was appalled when he was informed that there were rumors he had helped slaves escape to Canada, telling his former law partner Nathan Hall that such a charge was "too infamous to justify a denial" and was patently false "in fact and inference." He indignantly asserted, "I should as soon think of denying the charge as robbing a hen house." But then Fillmore asked that this denial be conveyed to General Taylor.[7] Fillmore's response accurately illustrates his views on this issue. Fillmore believed that anyone who knew him would have known that he would *never* consider helping a fugitive slave.

On the central issue of the age—the spread of slavery into the territories—Fillmore privately, and evasively, wrote that he had never "been called upon to express" his views on the Wilmot Proviso "in any official or public capacity." However, to an Alabamian, he more directly stated that he "regarded slavery as an evil, but one in which the National Government had nothing to do. That by the Constitution of the United States, the whole power over that question was vested in the Several states."[8] With regard to the territories, this letter, which was circulated nationally, was either a total

non sequitur or an admission that he believed the national government had no power whatsoever to regulate slavery in the territories, and thus only at statehood could a jurisdiction ban or allow
slavery. Oddly, this was the position of Lewis Cass, the Democratic
candidate for president in 1848.

After the election Fillmore remained in Albany closing out his
affairs and negotiating with Thurlow Weed about who would be
the next U.S. senator from New York. Since the Whigs controlled the
state legislature, they would choose the senator. John A. Collier, who
had nominated Fillmore for vice president at the national convention, wanted the position. With the new vice president's blessing,
he might have had it. Certainly Fillmore owed Collier his support,
but Fillmore may also have felt he owed Weed, since Weed and
Seward had not opposed his nomination the way Webster had
opposed Lawrence's. Thus, Fillmore agreed to support Seward for
the Senate. Biographers of Fillmore insist that he was snookered by
Weed, who pledged to work with Fillmore but then broke the
pledge. Such an analysis is far too simplistic. Fillmore, after all,
betrayed Collier (who deserved his support) to make a deal with
Seward even though they fundamentally disagreed on the key issues
of slavery in the territories, fugitive slaves, black rights, and nativism. Fillmore clearly was making the deal that seemed best to him
at the time, even if in the end Seward opposed him in the Senate
and in New York politics. It is also entirely possible that Fillmore
lacked the clout to block Seward's bid for the Senate and made the
best of the situation. In late February 1849, Fillmore, Weed, and
Seward shared a dinner that one Fillmore biographer describes as a
"love-fest," with all three men promising to work closely to share
patronage in the state.[9] The agreement fell apart almost as soon as
Fillmore arrived in Washington. Seward quickly maneuvered to
become one of Taylor's key advisers, gaining patronage for his own
supporters in New York, to Fillmore's great frustration. However,
these conflicts were ultimately about more than patronage. The
slaveholding Taylor turned out to be far closer to the antislavery

Seward than the doughface Fillmore on the central issues of the moment: slavery in the territories and California statehood.

At the end of February, Fillmore finally left Albany for Washington and the vice presidency. He journeyed alone. Abigail, suffering from various ailments, returned to Buffalo, where she remained throughout most of her husband's vice presidency. Fillmore arrived in Washington almost on the eve of the inauguration and finally met the president-elect for the first time. That this was their first meeting underscores the oddity of Fillmore's nomination.[10] Taylor had been a longtime figure in the military and, as such, was well known. Fillmore was essentially an unknown quantity—and an unknown person. His four terms as a congressman hardly made him a national figure. A general like Taylor would have met senior members of Congress throughout his long career, which had begun during Thomas Jefferson's administration, but Fillmore was never important enough for any general to encounter.

It is hard to know what either man expected of the other. Taylor was, after all, the first president who had never held any political office, elective or appointive, before becoming president.[11] He had no civilian political experience and virtually no nonmilitary experience. He owned plantations and slaves but managed them mostly as an absentee landowner. He had entered the army in 1808, when Fillmore was only eight years old, and had remained in the army until just before he ran for president. Although he had always favored the Whigs, he was not a Whig politician. Fillmore wanted to make sure Taylor supported the party's interests, but Fillmore was essentially a local politician, who even as vice president (and later as president) remained deeply interested in controlling patronage in New York. He also wanted to guide the political novice who was now president, but given Fillmore's relative lack of national experience, other party members must have wondered who would guide Fillmore. Meanwhile, Taylor conceived of himself as a president "above party," though it is not clear what he meant by this.

Shortly after the inauguration on March 5 (Taylor did not want to take the oath on March 4 because it was a Sunday), it became clear that Fillmore would be neither Taylor's confidant nor his adviser. That role would be played—to Fillmore's consternation—by New York's new U.S. senator William Henry Seward. Like Fillmore, Seward had impeccable Whig credentials. But Seward had a stronger power base in New York, where he had twice been governor. Even more important, he had greater contacts and connections outside of the state. Seward was a brilliant lawyer, a smart political tactician, and a national figure with far more political experience than Fillmore. He was backed by Thurlow Weed, the most powerful Whig newspaper editor in the nation's largest state. Seward was close to a number of men in the cabinet, especially Secretary of State John M. Clayton of Delaware and Secretary of the Navy William B. Preston of Virginia. Seward's superb social and political skills led to personal and political alliances with slave owners like Preston, Clayton, and the president, even though he never hid his antislavery views. Fillmore, on the other hand, socially awkward and lacking in self-confidence, made no friends and secured no allies in the new cabinet or the administration.

Seward did not control all the patronage in New York, but he had more influence than the vice president. Fillmore was able to help fill some patronage positions but not many. He failed to obtain a presidential appointment to West Point for the son of one of his friends. More disappointing, he was unable to get a patronage position for his longtime protégé, friend, and former law partner Nathan K. Hall. Hall was famously hostile to Seward, and this may be why Fillmore could not get Hall appointed to any position.[12] Thus, Fillmore remained an oddity, cut off from political power and terribly lonely, living at the Willard Hotel, a few blocks from the White House.[13] Abigail came to stay for a while but then returned to Buffalo, leaving her husband alone, professionally isolated and personally miserable.

Fillmore's biographers argue that the wily Seward sabotaged Fillmore by dealing directly with Taylor. One scholar condemns this alleged betrayal of Fillmore because "by temperament and conviction" the vice president "was in complete harmony with Taylor's cabinet."[14] This assessment is simply incorrect. Taylor confronted three pressing issues: the admission of California to the Union, the status of slavery in the new territories, and demands emanating from Austin that much of the New Mexico Territory be made part of Texas. Seward, like Taylor, favored immediately admitting California as a free state, keeping slavery out of the Mexican Cession, and resisting Texas's encroachment on New Mexico. Fillmore took the exact opposite position on all three issues. On the crucial issue of fugitive slaves, Fillmore and Taylor were also on opposite sides. Taylor (like Seward) saw no need for a stronger fugitive slave law; Fillmore vigorously supported this southern demand.

The most dramatic example of Fillmore's lack of "harmony" with Taylor came just before the president's unexpected death. In the summer of 1850 Congress was debating Henry Clay's omnibus bill, which would eventually lead to the Compromise of 1850. For a number of reasons, Taylor opposed the bill and was prepared to veto it. The vote in the Senate was expected to be extremely close, and Fillmore believed he might have to break a tie. Despite the president's opposition to the bill, Fillmore informed Taylor that if he had to break a tie vote, he would support the bill because he "deemed it for the interest of the country."[15] That Fillmore was prepared to vote against the position of his own administration indicates how much he was, and always had been, an outsider. Clearly, Fillmore was emphatically *not* in harmony with the president. He was fully prepared to embarrass Taylor by voting for the omnibus bill and in effect challenging his president.

Could Fillmore have had a happier, more congenial vice presidency? It might have been different if Fillmore himself had been a different person. He wanted to challenge Seward and Weed for leadership of the Whig Party in New York, but he was unable to articulate to Taylor the complexities of New York politics. Taylor may never have fully understood just how much bad blood there was between Seward and Fillmore, and thus he did not see how accepting Seward's recommendations for New York patronage undermined his own vice president. Fillmore, always unsure of himself and always conscious of his background and his inadequacies, was simply unable or unwilling to explain to the president of the United States—who was also an impressive war hero—the vulnerability of his own situation.

It is also possible that it would not have mattered. Unless there was a tie vote in the Senate, Taylor did not need Fillmore to accomplish his own political goals, and Fillmore was from the beginning openly at odds with Taylor on the big issues. Had Taylor been a more skilled politician, he might have been able to woo Fillmore, whose own insecurities would have made him open to such an approach. Similarly, had Fillmore been a more secure man and a better politician, he might have been able to outmaneuver Seward and work his way into Taylor's inner circle. Ironically, Fillmore was too insecure to be forceful and too proud to ingratiate himself with the president. The result was a deeply unhappy vice presidency.

· · ·

Fillmore's alienation from the administration might not have mattered, except that Taylor entered office facing an unprecedented crisis. Since the introduction of the Wilmot Proviso, national politics had been frozen over the status of slavery in the new territories, stimulated by heated rhetoric and talk of secession from the most extreme southern nationalists. Although a new Congress had been chosen by the time Taylor took office, its first session would not begin until the following December. This gave the administration time to develop a plan for solving the issues facing the nation. In the nine months from his inauguration until the new session of Congress, Taylor also had to make numerous patronage appointments. With the exception of Harrison's one month in office before his death in 1841, the Whigs had never held the presidency. Thus, scores of Whig politicians, desperate to obtain some office, inundated Taylor while he was trying to sort out how to settle the crisis.

The question of slavery in the territories was complicated by four other issues: (1) demands for immediate statehood for California since the gold rush had brought a flood of people into that far western territory; (2) increasing threats from the state of Texas to invade the New Mexico Territory; (3) growing northern opposition to the public sale of slaves in Washington, D.C.; and (4) southern dissatisfaction with the existing Fugitive Slave Act of 1793. Growing southern nationalism and threats of secession from radical southern politicians exacerbated these issues. In October 1849 southerners meeting in Jackson, Mississippi, had called for a convention of the southern states in Nashville the following June to consider the state of the Union. Many of them hoped the June meeting would result in calls for secession.

Since the end of the Mexican War, in 1848, there had been no formal territorial government in California. This was true for New Mexico and Utah as well, but those places had fewer settlers. The discovery of gold in December 1848 changed the dynamics, as tens of thousands of gold seekers poured into California. The 1850 census, completed later that year, would find more than ninety thousand people there, giving California a larger population than either Florida or Delaware—and this was probably a vast undercount. By the summer of 1850 everyone knew that California had a huge population with more settlers arriving daily, and an accurate census was impossible. Statehood was both necessary and just, and Taylor insisted that California be immediately admitted to the Union. Because there were relatively few slaves in the territory, all Americans assumed it would come in as a free state. Taylor also believed that New Mexico deserved statehood. Immediate statehood for these two territories would have preempted the debate over the Wilmot Proviso and strengthened the Union.

New Mexico statehood would also have solved the Texas boundary issue. Since the end of the Mexican War, the state government in Texas had been making extravagant claims to much of present-day New Mexico, including the city of Santa Fe. Even before Taylor's election, the residents of New Mexico had petitioned Congress to create a territorial government there. In September 1849 the

New Mexicans sent another petition to Washington, again asking to be organized as a territory. There had been no gold rush in New Mexico, but with more than sixty thousand residents, none of whom were slaves, it had a larger free population than Florida. New Mexico was certainly in a position to be admitted to the Union, which Taylor urged, along with California statehood, in his first annual message to Congress. Meanwhile, the president maintained an American military presence in New Mexico with every intention of standing up to the grandiose claims of the government in Austin, just as, in a different context, Andrew Jackson had been prepared to use military force to stand up to the extravagant claims of South Carolina about the meaning of federal law during the Nullification Crisis of 1832–33.

Taylor did not consider the District of Columbia slave trade a pressing issue. However, for more than a decade northerners had complained about the stain of human bondage, and especially the slave trade, in the nation's capital. In December 1848, at the beginning of the second session of the Thirtieth Congress, the House passed, on a mostly sectional vote, a resolution by the Whig congressman Daniel Gott of New York to have a committee draft legislation to end the slave trade in the District. The passage of this resolution embarrassed and angered the southern Whigs. A month later, John Wentworth, an Illinois Democrat, successfully moved to table Gott's resolution. However, Wentworth's Illinois colleague, the first-term Whig Abraham Lincoln, offered a substitute motion to begin a process of gradual abolition of slavery in the District, later announcing that he would propose a gradual abolition bill. But he never did, explaining, "I was abandoned by my former backers," so the bill had no chance of passing.[16] These proposals—especially when paired with the Wilmot Proviso—indicated growing northern demands that Congress regulate slavery where it had the power to do so: in the District of Columbia and the territories.

The fugitive slave issue had been simmering for years but had intensified after 1830 as new transportation systems—better roads, steamboats, and railroads—made it easier for slaves to escape. For example, in 1839 the soon to be famous fugitive slave Frederick Douglass simply boarded a train in Baltimore and headed north using papers borrowed from a free black sailor. The Constitution provided that the free states could not emancipate fugitive slaves. Instead, the fugitives were "to be delivered up on Claim from the Party to whom such Service or Labour may be due." The Constitution did not specify *who* would deliver the fugitive slave, and there was no debate on it at the Constitutional Convention. In 1793 Congress passed the first Fugitive Slave Act, which provided that all state and federal judges had jurisdiction to hear cases from masters who found and claimed their fugitive slaves. The law provided almost no due process protections for alleged fugitives and envisioned a summary proceeding.[17] Many northerners believed this act was unconstitutional because the Constitution did not authorize Congress to pass such a statute. Starting in the 1820s, almost every northern state passed a statute—generally known as a personal liberty law—to give greater due process protections for people seized as fugitive slaves. Pennsylvania's personal liberty law of 1826 made it a felony to remove a black person from the state without a certificate granted by a state judge, and it imposed a far tougher standard of proof than the federal law required. The personal liberty laws were designed to prevent kidnapping, which happened often enough to make many northern blacks live in fear. However, southern masters complained that the laws hampered the return of fugitive slaves. By the late 1830s and early 1840s, there was significant hostility in much of the North to the return of fugitive slaves. Moderate nonabolitionist chief justices in New York and New Jersey declared the 1793 act unconstitutional, while Pennsylvania's highest court upheld that state's personal liberty law. Some southerners sought to avoid fugitive slave hearings by securing indictments for theft, arguing that their missing slaves had stolen the clothing they were wearing when they ran away. Southern governors then tried to extradite these blacks, but northern governors, including William H. Seward in New York, routinely refused to recognize these bogus demands. Similarly, Seward and his Maine counterparts also refused to return sailors to Virginia and Georgia after they helped slaves escape from those states. These northern governors denied that helping a slave escape constituted a crime, because no one could own another person.[18]

The issue of fugitive slaves reached a crisis in the aftermath of the Supreme Court's ruling in *Prigg v. Pennsylvania* (1842) that all of the northern personal liberty laws were unconstitutional and that the free states could not require any additional proof beyond what the 1793 federal law mandated. In addition, the Court held that masters had a common law right to seize their fugitive "property" and bring their slaves home without any judicial hearing at all, as long as it was done without a "breach of the peace." This ruling undermined black freedom in Pennsylvania, New Jersey, and along the Ohio River, and it seemed to be an open invitation for kidnapping at night when no one might notice the violent seizure of a free black person. While prohibiting the free states from interfering with the return of a fugitive slave, the Court also held that the free states could not be required to enforce the federal law. Thus, a year after *Prigg*, officials in Boston refused to incarcerate the fugitive slave George Latimer while his master waited for paperwork to arrive. In the end, the Virginia owner freed Latimer after receiving a small sum as "payment." Shortly after that, Massachusetts passed the "Latimer Law," officially prohibiting all law enforcement officials in the state from participating in the return of fugitive slaves. Other free states passed similar laws. In *Jones v. Van Zandt* (1847), the Supreme Court upheld an enormous judgment against an Ohio abolitionist who was sued after he offered a ride in his wagon to a group of blacks walking along the road outside of Cincinnati. Van Zandt, a poor farmer, claimed he had no notice they were slaves, but the court rejected this argument, essentially holding that northerners should assume that blacks might be fugitives and not help them travel in the North. William H. Seward represented Van Zandt before the U.S. Supreme Court.[19]

By the time Taylor took office, partisans on both sides of the Mason-Dixon line were deeply unhappy about the problem of fugitive slaves. Northerners hated the idea of slave catchers roaming their states and feared that free blacks would be taken south and enslaved. Such fears were not unfounded. At least one of the alleged slaves removed to Maryland by Edward Prigg had been born free in Pennsylvania, but that did not seem to bother the Supreme Court. On the other hand, southerners complained that the Constitution gave them a right to recover their runaway slaves and that the North was not cooperating in the process. Indeed, the issue of fugitive slave returns had flipped the usual ideological categories. Northerners asserted states' rights arguments to protect free blacks and fugitive slaves, while southerners demanded strict enforcement of their constitutional rights and a strong national government imposing its will on the northern states.

When the Thirty-first Congress convened in December 1849, all of these issues came to a head. Taylor hoped to deal with them piecemeal, starting with the immediate admission of California and then New Mexico. In the meantime, he was prepared to authorize a strong military response to any attempts by Texas to invade New Mexico. His model was another slaveholding former general, President Andrew Jackson, who had been prepared to use troops to stop nullification. It is not clear how Taylor wanted to deal with the slave trade in Washington, D.C., or the issue of fugitive slaves, but as a soldier who had served in the North as well as the South—and commanded men from each region—Taylor understood the necessity of compromise and recognition of the needs of both.

Had the Whigs in Congress backed Taylor, it is possible the crisis would have been averted. But they were unwilling to follow their own president. Henry Clay and Daniel Webster were still smarting over their failure to win the presidential nomination in 1848. Neither of these longtime Whig leaders could quite understand how they had been denied the presidency by an upstart general with no political experience. Clay in particular wanted to step into what he saw as a leadership vacuum and assume command of the party from the Senate.

In a sense, neither Clay nor Webster could figure out what their role should be now that a Whig lived in the White House. They distrusted Taylor, had only barely tolerated his election, and would not work with him. Since the formation of the Whig Party, these men had mostly been in the opposition. They knew how to fight against a Democratic president; they had done so for most of their careers. Unfortunately, they did not know how to work with a president of their own party. Thus, Clay, with the cooperation of Webster, planned his own solution to the crisis. Fillmore, who presided over the Senate, quickly sided with Clay and Webster. When he was a freshman congressman, Webster had befriended Fillmore, and Fillmore had not forgotten this. As a longtime Whig, Fillmore respected and admired Clay. Moreover, supporting Clay and Webster was a vehicle for opposing Seward, who remained the vice president's nemesis. The stage was set for one of the great legislative debates in American history: the arguments over the Compromise of 1850.

·   ·   ·

The origin of the Compromise of 1850 and the debate over it in the Senate is an iconic moment of American history. On what was literally a dark and stormy night in late January 1850, Henry Clay surreptitiously visited Daniel Webster to discuss the compromise. The two giants of the Whig Party secretly agreed to cooperate on a compromise that they believed would save the Union. The plan was designed to outflank southern extremists, such as John C. Calhoun, who were trying to create a "southern" party that would force slave-state Whigs to align with them and bring about a fundamental restructuring of American politics. Most southern Whigs rejected this move, correctly seeing it as mostly about Calhoun's own desires for political power and his wish to undermine a Whig president. But, while fighting off Calhoun and his southern allies, Clay was equally interested in undermining Taylor's presidency. Clay wanted to save the nation, but he also hoped to make himself the most powerful member of his party in the process.

On January 29, 1850, Clay presented his eight resolutions to the Senate.[20] His goal was to have a single bill that would attract votes from both sections. Five of the eight provisions directly benefited the South: a new fugitive slave law, organization of the new territories "without the adoption of any restriction or condition on the subject of slavery," federal assumption of the debt that the Republic of Texas had when it entered the Union, an ironclad proclamation that Congress could never end slavery in the District of Columbia without the support of the people of the District and state of Maryland, and, finally, another resolution affirming that Congress would never interfere with the interstate slave trade. The three resolutions he offered the North would immediately admit California as a free state, prohibit the public sale of slaves in the District of Columbia, and settle the Texas boundary dispute somewhat, but not wholly, in favor of New Mexico. However, the value of the proposal to the North was quite problematic.

The most divisive aspect of the compromise measures was the new fugitive slave law. Before turning to that law, it is important to understand how one-sided Clay's compromise was. The great gain for the North was the admission of California as a free state. However, with nearly a hundred thousand people, almost no slaves, and a population expanding at a record pace, it was impossible to imagine any other outcome. Southerners eyed California, where slaves could be used in mines and in the region's fertile valleys. In its first decade of statehood there would be a number of attempts to bring some form of slavery into California.[21] But in 1850 only about 1 percent of the population was black, and many of these individuals were free. Whatever southerners might have wanted, California clearly would not be a slave state. Thus, Clay's compromise "gave" to the North what it already had: the free state of California. The compromise banned "the slave trade, in slaves brought into" the District "from states or places beyond the District, either to be sold as merchandise or to be transported to other markets without the District of Columbia." This proposed law would remove a visible irritant that tended to fan antislavery sentiment, but it would have absolutely no effect on slavery itself. Indeed, a shrewd defender of slavery might have concluded that the proposal would actually reduce the growth of antislavery sentiment by removing an aggravating practice that was always in the face of antislavery members of Congress without actually harming slavery. Masters could still buy and sell slaves privately, and they could still ship them out of the District for sale farther south. The slave market in Alexandria, Virginia, which was just across the river from the District, also remained open to them. Thus, this piece of the compromise did not harm slavery or undermine its viability in the District. In fact, it might have had the opposite effect.

Clay's proposal for the settlement of the New Mexico boundary was also of dubious benefit to the North. The proposal offered Texas less land than it wanted, and this would prevent the further growth of that vast empire for slavery. But the land not ceded to Texas would simply remain part of the New Mexico Territory, where, under Clay's proposal, slavery would be allowed. If the Wilmot Proviso had been adopted, then slavery would have been banned in the new territories, making the debate over the New Mexico boundary more important, because every acre not given to Texas would remain free soil. However, Clay's proposals were a shell game. He first offered to add only a little land to Texas, which would presumably please the North, but then he opened all of New Mexico to slavery. Implicitly, this meant that slavery would be allowed in the new territories, and southerners surely expected these places would become slave states.

In the long run, had the Civil War not intervened, Clay's proposed settlement of the New Mexico–Texas land issue might actually have helped slavery. Texas wanted about half of present-day New Mexico. If this had occurred, then the remaining territory would probably have come into the Union as one single slave state. By guaranteeing that the New Mexico Territory would be very large—consisting of present-day Arizona and New Mexico and some of present-day Texas—Clay's proposed settlement of the border dispute actually benefited the South. With more than 200,000 square miles, this territory was about four times the size of the most recent state (Wisconsin) to enter the Union and might have provided three or more slave states.

Most scholars have failed to understand that the remaining compromise measures wholly benefited the South.[22] In addition to taking the Wilmot Proviso off the table, which in itself was a major victory for the South, Clay's compromise also substantially undercut the Missouri Compromise. Much of the Mexican Cession—the present-day states of Nevada and Utah, as well as most of Colorado and a bit of Wyoming—lay north of the 36°30′ line. Clay's compromise actually vitiated the Missouri Compromise line by opening over 180,000 square miles to slavery north of that line. This vast space was more than four times the size of North Carolina, four times the size of Tennessee, and six times the size of South Carolina—in other words, large enough to accommodate several new slave states. If Clay had been truly interested in a compromise, he would have followed the 1820 line, thus giving some of the new territory to the North and some to the South. Instead, with the exception of California, which was out of his control, he gave all the new territories to the South.

By opening all the new territories to slavery and refusing to apply the Missouri Compromise line to the new territory, Clay completely undermined the value to the free states of settling the New Mexico–Texas boundary in favor of New Mexico. Clay then compounded this issue by giving Texas a vast sum of money—the first federal bailout of a state—to pay off its prestatehood debts. This money would come from the general revenues, thus guaranteeing that northern taxpayers would substantially contribute to the Texas bailout.

The two resolutions on slavery in the District of Columbia and on the interstate slave trade were also major victories for supporters of slavery, especially when seen in the light of all of Clay's resolutions.[23] Except for a few abolitionists who were well outside the mainstream of their own movement, most opponents of slavery agreed that Congress had no power to regulate slavery in the states where it existed. Political opponents of slavery in the 1850s agreed that there were essentially five areas where Congress could regulate slavery. The first was the African slave trade, which had been banned in 1808 and was not an issue in 1850. The second was in the territories, where Congress had the power to ban slavery. Clay's compromise measures would preempt that by opening *all* of the remaining new territories to slavery. The third was the regulation of the District of Columbia, where Congress had specific and plenary power under the Constitution to "exercise exclusive Legislation in all Cases."[24] Under this power the compromise measures allowed Congress to end the public sale of slaves there. But, in Clay's other resolution on the District, Congress voluntarily ceded its powers over the District to the people who lived there *and* to the state of Maryland. Never before (or since) had Congress been asked to promise never to exercise one of its constitutionally enumerated powers without first getting the approval of a single state to act. The fourth area of congressional regulation concerned the interstate slave trade. The Constitution gave Congress complete power to regulate commerce "among the several States,"[25] which included the interstate slave trade. Under Clay's resolution, Congress would promise never to exercise the power that it had. This was an unprecedented abdication of congressional power. It was also a direct assault on antislavery constitutionalism, by essentially telling political opponents of slavery that they *could never* get Congress to exercise its well-recognized powers on behalf of freedom.

The fifth area of congressional power concerned the return of fugitive slaves. Many constitutional scholars and jurists had argued that Congress did not have a role to play here, but the Supreme Court had settled this issue in favor of congressional power and the South in *Prigg v. Pennsylvania*. If Congress had plenary power to regulate the return of fugitive slaves, then it could do so in a variety of ways. Clay did not spell out any details in his resolutions; that came later. But the eventual law—the Fugitive Slave Act of 1850— would be an enormous legislative victory for what northerners called "the slave power." It would create the first national system of law enforcement, and it would deny alleged fugitives—including free blacks wrongly claimed as fugitive slaves—fundamental due process rights.

Historians have always assumed that the admission of California was a major victory for the North, because it gave the free states a permanent majority in the Senate. But this is the wisdom of hindsight. A number of times before 1850, one section or the other had had a majority in the Senate. Most historians write about the "pairing" of southern and northern territories in admitting new states. This in fact rarely happened. For six years in the 1790s there was a majority of free states. From 1803 (when Ohio was admitted) until 1812 (when Louisiana entered), there was a also free-state majority. The South gained a two-state majority in 1845 with the admissions of Arkansas and Texas, which was reduced a year later to one state with the admission of Iowa. The South retained this one-state majority until 1848. Thus, there was no reason to believe that California would create a permanent free-state majority, especially since Clay's resolutions allowed slavery in New Mexico and Utah, with nearly 400,000 square miles to be divided into slave states.

From February until July 4, the Senate debated these measures. The debates were some of the most eloquent and memorable in American history. On March 7, Webster surprised the nation—and lost almost all credibility in his home state—by supporting the compromise resolutions. He poignantly told his colleagues: "I wish to speak to-day, not as a Massachusetts man, nor as a Northern man, but as an American." He urged passage of the compromise measures to save the Union, even though he was abandoning all his previous opposition to spreading slavery into the territories and ignoring the very real threats to the black community in his own state from the proposed fugitive slave law. Webster may have spoken "as an American," but he also spoke as a Whig who was bitter that he had never been his party's presidential candidate and who was hostile to one of the most successful candidates his party had ever fielded. Like Clay, he wanted to save the Union while also empowering himself and perhaps finally getting to the White House.

John C. Calhoun, Jefferson Davis, James Mason, and other

southern fire-eaters opposed the compromise. Calhoun asked for a fundamental restructuring of the constitutional arrangements, to give the South a permanent veto over any legislation proposed in Congress. Staunch opponents of slavery such as Seward, Chase, and Hannibal Hamlin of Maine also denounced the compromise. Speaking as a man who had defended black rights for his whole career, Seward declared the compromise was "radically wrong and essentially vicious, involving the surrender of the exercise of judgment and conscience." Taylor was unhappy with the self-righteousness of Seward's speech, but he was not entirely in disagreement with Seward's complaints that the compromise gave too much to slavery and rejected American values of liberty and fundamental justice.[26] Taylor wanted immediate admission of California, followed by statehood for New Mexico. He did not really believe Texas would force a confrontation over the sands of eastern New Mexico, but Old Rough and Ready ordered troops to New Mexico to be ready and, if necessary, rough in enforcing the sovereignty of the United States against a renegade state. Taylor opposed opening the Southwest to slavery, and he had no interest in tying the admission of California to a new fugitive slave law. Clay nevertheless moved forward in opposition to the president of his party.

The Senate debates over the compromise continued through the spring. At times they were nasty and even violent. In April, Senator Henry S. Foote of Mississippi pulled a pistol on Senator Thomas Hart Benton of Missouri, but calm was finally restored without shots being fired. Vice President Fillmore, presiding over the Senate, watched in horror, but he was unable to rein in any senator's vituperative language or penchant for near violence. While a handful of senators, mostly from the South, successfully undermined Fillmore's ability to control tempers or even provide a measure of decorum, the dignified Clay continued to push for his compromise. But while Clay hoped to save the Union, he also directly challenged Taylor's leadership. On May 21 he openly attacked Taylor, saying that the Whig president's plan would not solve the crisis but would lead the country to "bleed more profusely than ever."[27]

Despite the nastiness and the near violence, the debates continued and in the process undermined the most hotheaded southerners. In June the Nashville Convention, which was the brainchild of
the fire-eaters, fizzled as only seven of the fifteen slave states sent
an official delegation. The call for the convention had been biparti-
san, but only Democrats, and extremist Democrats at that, showed
up in June. Significantly, these southern radicals passed a resolution
that called only for the extension of the 36°30' parallel through the
Mexican Cession, giving New Mexico, Arizona, and southern California to the South and Utah and Nevada to the North. They did
not have the audacity to demand access to all of the Mexican Cession, even though Clay was prepared to give it to them. The convention then adjourned, with plans to meet in the fall after the
session of Congress was over.

Throughout this period, Vice President Fillmore supported Clay
and the compromise, telling Taylor that if he had to break a tie in
the Senate he would do so in favor of Clay's bill. Assuming Clay's
bill also passed the House, this would have forced Taylor to veto
the compromise, which would have undermined his administration.[28] Fillmore apparently had no compunctions about embarrassing Taylor.

That was where the debate stood when Congress recessed for
the Fourth of July holiday. A week later Zachary Taylor was dead.
Millard Fillmore, the most obscure vice president ever, was now
president of the United States.

4

The New President

On July 10, 1850, Millard Fillmore went to the House of Representatives to take the oath of office as president of the United States. Eighty-one-year-old William Cranch, the chief judge for the Circuit Court of the District of Columbia, administered the oath. Cranch, appointed by President John Adams in 1801, was the last surviving Federalist officeholder, and Fillmore doubtless appreciated this tie to the Founding Fathers. The mood was somber. There were no speeches. Fillmore told Margaret Taylor she could stay in the White House as long as she needed, but within three days the president's widow had moved out. Shortly thereafter Fillmore moved in, and in the fall Abigail, who had last visited her husband in March, returned to Washington.[1]

On the day he took the oath of office, all of the members of the cabinet tendered their resignations to President Fillmore as a pro forma courtesy to their new boss; all of them expected to continue in their posts. Taylor's cabinet had been filled with loyal Whigs who were moderate on all the issues of the day. Secretary of the Interior Thomas Ewing and Secretary of State John Clayton were major figures in the party. Attorney General Reverdy Johnson was a highly respected constitutional lawyer.

Fillmore had not been close to Taylor's cabinet; like most vice presidents, he had been shunted off to the side. In this era, the vice president was never considered part of the president's cabinet and was not usually invited to cabinet meetings.[2] Taylor and his cabinet had never considered Fillmore to be part of the inner circle, as was the case for virtually every vice president until the middle of the twentieth century.[3]

Fillmore, however, seems to have been particularly wounded by Taylor's failure to include him. His inexperience and his lifelong sense of insecurity no doubt made it especially hard for him to be a vice president with no role to play in the administration. And so he acted impulsively upon becoming president. The usually careful, plodding Fillmore reverted to the petulant teenager who had stormed off from his first legal apprenticeship. Angry that the cabinet members had not included him in their deliberations, he fired the entire cabinet—an act that astounded them along with the leaders of the Whig Party. Even more astonishing, after firing all of the cabinet members, Fillmore asked them to stay on for a month as the new administration got off the ground. Not surprisingly, the stunned and doubtlessly furious cabinet officers refused.

. . .

Fillmore is the only "accidental president" to have summarily removed the entire cabinet of his predecessor. John Tyler, even more of an outsider than Fillmore, kept William Henry Harrison's cabinet for much of his term. Andrew Johnson, an outsider in the Lincoln administration, initially kept most of Lincoln's cabinet. Although Lyndon Johnson felt abused and rejected by John F. Kennedy and his team, Johnson nevertheless retained a significant number of Kennedy's cabinet members, not only for the rest of the term but into his own term as well. Fillmore, however, rid himself of Taylor's entire team on the first day of his presidency. Still a novice on the national political scene, he was suddenly without any advisers or even department heads to help run the country. He was, however, in constant conversation with numerous political leaders, especially Daniel Webster. On July 20, ten days after taking the oath of office, Fillmore sent nominations to the Senate for some cabinet positions. He clearly had not had much time to think about these appointments, consult with party leaders, or seek advice beyond people who were already in Washington.

Fillmore's decision to fire the entire cabinet reflected a stubbornness that profoundly affected his presidency. His eventual secretary of the interior, Alexander H. H. Stuart, noted that "when he had carefully examined a question & had satisfied himself that he was right, no power on earth, could induce him to swerve from what he believed to be the line of duty."[4] This stubbornness would reemerge in Fillmore's unswerving support for the Fugitive Slave Act and his relentless prosecution of its opponents.

Daniel Webster became the new secretary of state and Fillmore's closest adviser. At one level, this was a superb choice. Webster had been first elected to the House of Representatives in 1813 and had been in either the House or the Senate for most of his life. He had also served as secretary of state under Harrison and Tyler. He was a distinguished constitutional lawyer who had argued numerous landmark cases before the Supreme Court, and he had a well-earned reputation as a passionate and brilliant speaker. His "Reply to Hayne" in the nullification debate of 1830 was one of the great speeches of the age, and it is still cited for its ringing endorsement of "Liberty and Union, now and forever, one and inseparable." He had sought the presidency for two decades; at sixty-eight he was an elder statesman of the party and, Fillmore must have thought, unlikely to challenge him for the Whig Party's presidential nomination in 1852. Instead, Webster was now in a position to help salvage the first real Whig presidency since William Henry Harrison spent one month in the White House before his untimely death in 1841.

Webster also had a reputation for greed and, if not corruption, then at least an unprincipled willingness to sell himself and his talents to the highest bidder. He accepted the cabinet appointment only after a group of Boston businessmen provided him with a salary supplement to offset the loss of income from practicing law, which as a senator he had continued to do. While not illegal or

completely unethical by the standards of the time, this was surely
unseemly. Smarmy though he was, Webster was a stalwart Whig
and a longtime power in the party, and his appointment might have
been a great asset to Fillmore, had it occurred before his famous
Seventh of March speech in favor of Clay's compromise. But after
that speech, Webster had become a pariah in the North, especially
in his home state of Massachusetts. He had lost almost all credibility with his constituents. The antislavery poet John Greenleaf
Whittier wrote of Webster in his poem "Ichabod":

> So fallen! so lost! the light withdrawn
> Which once he wore!
> The glory from his gray hairs gone
> Forevermore!

By the summer of 1850 Webster was indeed a fallen angel in the
North. Once an icon of Free Soil, he was willing to give up everything the North stood for in order to appease the insatiable demands
of the slavocracy, hoping it would help make him president. His
constituents would have no part of him. His term would have ended
after the 1850 election, and he had little chance of being returned
to the Senate. Thus, Fillmore rescued Webster by bringing him
into the cabinet. The move once again illustrates Fillmore's utter
inability to understand the deep hatred of slavery among huge numbers of northerners. Probably no other appointment undermined
Fillmore in his own backyard more than making Webster the most
important member of his cabinet. As secretary of state, Webster
became fanatical about enforcing the new Fugitive Slave Act, sug-
gesting that he no longer believed that "liberty " and "union" were
inseparable but that he was willing and even eager to sacrifice liberty for union, especially if it would lead to a presidential nomination. His obsession with enforcing the Fugitive Slave Act would
only confirm Whittier's judgment that Webster had become an
"ichabod"—one who is inglorious.

Fillmore's choice for secretary of the Treasury, Thomas Corwin, had been a U.S. senator from Ohio and a major player in that state's Whig Party. He had opposed the Mexican War as an unnecessary war of aggression but had not supported the Wilmot Proviso and had taken no particular stand on slavery.[5] Like Fillmore, he was hostile to the antislavery movement, which he considered an annoyance that undermined nationalism and the chance for the Whigs to implement their economic policies. The Kentuckian John J. Crittenden, the new attorney general, had been a senator and governor. Like Webster, he now held the same position in Fillmore's cabinet that he had held under Harrison. He was a safe Whig and a slaveholding southerner who would support the compromise and oppose the antislavery wing of the party. William Graham of North Carolina, who became secretary of the navy, had also been in the Senate. He too was a conservative Whig.[6]

On July 22 and 23, the Senate confirmed all of these men, along with Fillmore's choice for postmaster general, his former law partner Nathan K. Hall. In addition to being Fillmore's confidant, Hall was also notorious in New York for his open hostility to Seward and Weed. The postmaster general controlled more patronage jobs than anyone else in the cabinet, because he could remove and appoint all the local postmasters in the country. The post office was also the government department most susceptible to corruption because its employees handled huge amounts of cash. It made sense to put a trusted ally and friend in this position, since when Fillmore ran for election on his own in 1852 he wanted an army of sympathetic postmasters spread across the nation ready to work for him.

Fillmore's haste in firing Taylor's cabinet left him without a secretary of war[7] until mid-August and without a secretary of the interior until September. At least three men, including Edward Bates of Missouri, declined Fillmore's request to head the War Department. This embarrassing fiasco underscores his impetuousness in firing Taylor's cabinet. With the nation mourning a dead president, a wiser, more politically sophisticated, and more personally secure man might have moved slowly, replacing the Taylor cabinet one secretary at a time, after first securing a replacement for each officer. But Fillmore did not do this, and so he spent six weeks searching for a secretary of war, until he finally persuaded Charles Conrad of Louisiana to take the job. Conrad, an utterly undistinguished and unknown Whig, had served one year in the Senate and in 1850 was in his first term in the House. He had no particular expertise with military issues. One of Zachary Taylor's early backers, Conrad had tried to persuade the late president to support Texas's claims to most of New Mexico. Conrad had only two assets: he was a moderate southern Whig and he was willing to accept the appointment.[8]

Fillmore took even longer, more than two months, to find a new secretary of the interior. When Senator James Pearce of Maryland declined the offer, Fillmore considered another Marylander, John Pendleton Kennedy, only to discover that his nomination would split the party in that state. He finally turned to Thomas McKennan of Pennsylvania, who, like Fillmore, had begun his career in Congress as a member of the Anti-Masonic Party. McKennan had not held office since 1843, so he had taken no position on any of the issues of the moment and therefore had not offended anyone. McKennan was finally confirmed on August 15, but he resigned a week later to become a railroad president. Fillmore was once again embarrassed by his haste in firing the cabinet and his inability to find, appoint, and retain a cabinet officer. He had to begin the search again, and he eventually persuaded Alexander H. H. Stuart of Virginia to take the post. Stuart had served a single term in Congress and had been a strong supporter of Henry Clay from the time he entered politics in the 1830s. Stuart was a moderate on slavery and turned out to be quite competent in organizing the new Department of the Interior, which had been created only in 1849.[9]

Because he insisted on removing all of Taylor's cabinet the same day he took office, Fillmore had less time than any other president in American history to form a cabinet. All elected presidents have had from the time of their election until their inauguration to do this. Every accidental president, except Fillmore, kept the existing cabinet and then gradually made changes. Some elected presidents have retained cabinet officers of their predecessors, even if they were of a different party.[10] Fillmore fired those in office, all loyal members of his own party, on the first day of his administration. Only then did he start the process of finding replacements. It was not an auspicious beginning.

• • •

As Fillmore struggled to fill his cabinet, the Senate continued to debate Clay's omnibus bill. Meanwhile, Fillmore faced his first crisis without the benefit of having his cabinet in place. Just a few days after he was sworn in, Fillmore received a letter from Governor Peter H. Bell of Texas—addressed to the now-deceased President Taylor—demanding that the United States recognize Texas's extravagant claims to much of New Mexico, including Santa Fe, and to disavow the U.S. Army's actions to preserve the integrity of the New Mexico Territory.

Bell's absurdly arrogant communication would probably have bemused Taylor, a commander in chief with vast military experience and with a full cabinet in place, including a secretary of war to deal with military issues and a secretary of the interior to deal with territorial questions. Indeed, Taylor was prepared to personally lead the army in New Mexico to stop an invasion of federal territory, just as Andrew Jackson had been prepared to march to South Carolina to suppress nullification nearly two decades earlier. Fillmore had no military experience, no secretary of war, no secretary of the interior, and no sense of the impossibility of Texas enforcing its will against a determined American president. Texas had a lot of land, very few people, and huge debts. More than 750 miles of mostly trackless desert and scrub lands separated Austin from Santa Fe. Experienced soldiers were stationed in New Mexico, and it would have been hard to imagine Texas successfully invading the territory. In August, Fillmore ordered an additional 750 soldiers to New Mexico. But despite his understanding that he needed to defend United States territory against an invasion from any source, Fillmore was ultimately unwilling to confront the Texans over their absurd territorial claims. Taylor had been ready to meet this argument head on. Fillmore vacillated. He sent more troops to New Mexico but then gave Texas almost everything it demanded.

Fillmore might have sent a stern response to Governor Bell, reminding him who was commander in chief, who had an army, and who did not. Or he might have sent him a lawyerly explanation of how the United States Constitution worked. He did neither. Nor did he move to bring New Mexico into the Union along with California, as Taylor had wanted. This would have preempted the Texas debate and mooted the Wilmot Proviso debate. By this time the residents of New Mexico had already held a convention and written a state constitution, which was on its way to Washington. Thus, statehood could have been quickly accomplished.

In their constitution, the New Mexicans made extravagant claims for their proposed state, based on the old Mexican Department of New Mexico, which would have moved the New Mexico boundary deep into what everyone agreed was clearly the state of Texas. Under the United States Constitution, no state could be forced to give up its own territory against its will. New Mexico's admission to the Union would thus have had to preserve the existing borders of Texas. Furthermore, a territory could never define its own boundaries. Only Congress could do that. The territorial claims of the New Mexico convention therefore had no basis in law, just as the Texas claims to territory acquired by the United States from Mexico were legally baseless.

These constitutional and legal realities created the potential for presidential leadership. A strong president could have firmly, but tactfully, told both sides they were wrong. Texas was in the Union with the boundaries Congress had already set; New Mexico could enter the Union with boundaries that Congress would create. Since New Mexico had a free population greater than Florida's, it was certainly entitled to admission into the Union. There were many variations on this strategy. Fillmore might have offered to support a compromise that would have admitted New Mexico as a free state under the theory of popular sovereignty that Lewis Cass had proposed in the 1848 election. The extreme southern hotheads were all Democrats, and they would have been forced to repudiate the principles of their own party if they objected to New Mexico statehood on this basis. Fillmore then might have urged that Congress pay off the bonds of the Republic of Texas, as Clay had proposed. He might even have offered a compromise on its land claims with New Mexico, as Clay had also proposed.[11] Or he might have forcefully sent Congress a concrete proposal for settling the boundary one way or the other.

Instead, Fillmore was so paralyzed by the Texans' saber rattling that he seems to have forgotten that he was both president and commander in chief. His leadership, if one could call it that, was to appease the Texas legislature by refusing to submit the proposed New Mexico constitution to Congress. He offered no guidance to Congress at this time, beyond indicating he supported Clay's omnibus bill, which was set to open up all of the Mexican Cession to slavery—despite the clear objections of the residents of New Mexico and the repudiation of the Missouri Compromise in Nevada and Utah.

With no leadership from the Whig in the White House, on July 24 the Democrats in the Senate proposed that Congress not actually set the New Mexico–Texas boundary but instead create a commission to do so. On the heels of this, a Georgia Whig, William Dawson, put together a coalition of southerners and northern Democrats to stipulate that until the commission met, the New Mexico territorial government would have no authority in the disputed area. This was patently unfair to the claims of New Mexico, and it led to a total unraveling of the compromise. A week later, on July 31, another Whig, James Pearce, who was a close ally of Fillmore, moved that the whole New Mexico issue be eliminated from the pending bill. A series of other amendments followed, and by the end of the day the compromise was dead.

The compromise had begun with Clay attempting to wrest control of the Whig Party from its own president. Clay envisioned he would once again be the party leader and hero of the nation, as he had been when he guided the Missouri Compromise through Congress in 1820. It might just, finally, make him president. But the strategy had backfired. In the Senate, the party had become utterly leaderless, with two Whigs—both of whom supported the compromise—amending the compromise to death while Clay looked on helplessly. The old president was dead, and thus there was no need for Clay to dethrone him. The new president, a long-standing Whig, offered no leadership on the nation's pressing issues. Clay, devastated by the collapse of all his work, left Washington even though Congress remained in session until September.

At this point, Senator Stephen A. Douglas, a Democrat from Illinois, began to put the compromise back together, with Fillmore pressuring the Whigs to go along. This was the ultimate irony of Clay's and Fillmore's machinations against Taylor. Designed to promote Clay and the regular Whigs, and to undermine Taylor, the compromise ended up catapulting the Democrat Douglas to greater prominence and would, in the end, devastate Fillmore's presidency.

Douglas broke the compromise into its component parts and guided them through Congress one at a time, with a small group of southern and northern senators and representatives voting for all, or almost all, the measures, and then picking up the rest of the southerners or northerners for particular issues. The new shaping of this legislation, as a series of separate and disconnected laws, undermined any pretense of an actual compromise between competing parties. If all the southerners supported a bill and only one northerner (Douglas) joined them, the bill would pass. Similarly, if all the northerners supported a bill, and just one southerner joined them, it too would pass. This outcome actually favored the South, because now that New Mexico statehood or the extension of the Missouri Compromise line to the Utah Territory were off the table, only two parts of the original compromise—California statehood and closing the public slave trade in Washington, D.C.—favored the North.

Thus, the final Compromise of 1850—which perhaps more correctly should be called the "Appeasement of 1850"—favored the South over the North and slavery over freedom.[12] All this was accomplished with the active support of a northern Whig president working closely with a northern Democratic senator to defeat the interests of other northern Whigs and some northern Democrats.

Fillmore's response to the demands of Texas illustrates his failure of leadership. Fillmore's August 6 special message to Congress on Texas was an almost total capitulation to Texas and its aggressive claims. Fillmore pointed out, correctly, that the dispute over the Texas boundary was not between New Mexico and Texas but between the government of the United States and Texas. He detailed the way the Constitution operated, pointed out that he had the power to call out the militia or army under some circumstances, and explained how the disputed land had been acquired by a treaty between the United States and Mexico. He asserted that if armed Texans entered New Mexico, they would not be doing so under color of law and that they would be "trespassers" and were to "be regarded merely as intruders."[13] This was odd terminology for what others might have called invaders, rebels, or even traitors. So far, except for his milquetoast description of invaders as "trespassers," Fillmore seemed to have learned the lessons of Andrew Jackson and Zachary Taylor when dealing with renegade states. Reading this part of the message, which he drew up in consultation with Webster, one might think that Webster was remembering his great confrontation with Senator Hayne over nullification.

But this initial strong response was just a prelude to Fillmore's appeasement of the Texans. Astoundingly, he then asserted that the "executive government of the United States has no power or authority" to determine what the boundary line of the United States was *before* President Polk signed the Treaty of Guadalupe Hidalgo. In other words, the president of the United States told the Congress that it was not his job to assert what the national boundaries were even though every president since George Washington had asserted strong plenary power over foreign policy. If this were really the case, then the president did not know where to collect foreign duties, when an invading army had entered the nation, or where to regulate immigration, if the nation chose to do so, as Fillmore's nativist allies wanted.[14] Fillmore, having just declared that only the Congress could determine what the boundary of the United States had been before 1848, then added that "the assent of the State of Texas may be necessary" to decide where the boundary was.[15] Thus, Fillmore and Webster decided unilaterally that Texas should have a veto power—a power of nullification—over the executive branch and Congress. Under Fillmore's bizarre theory, Congress could pass a law deciding what the boundaries of the New Mexico Territory were, and the president could sign this law, but Texas would have the right and the power to reject the result. Webster had apparently forgotten where he once stood on the question of nullification; Fillmore had apparently forgotten that the Constitution was the "supreme law of the land."

Fillmore's plan was to guide Congress in passing a law that the Texans would accept. The final settlement over the Southwest, which passed the Senate on August 9, gave Texas about seventy thousand square miles more than Clay's bill had (and took that territory away from New Mexico), opened up the entire New Mexico Territory to slavery, *and* gave Texas a $10 million bailout. The politics of this included a fear—perpetuated by Fillmore and Webster— that if the issues were not settled there would be civil war between Texas and the United States of America over who owned the New Mexico desert. Taylor, the general who had served in the region and knew the geography of Texas and New Mexico, would have thought this was preposterous. But Fillmore, without a working cabinet or a secretary of war and never having seen the vast deserts of the Southwest, was cowed by the idea that Texas could somehow raise an army that would be a match for that of the entire United States! Webster, now seemingly in control of White House patronage, pressured New England's Whig senators to accept the Texas bill. The Senate, led by Douglas, made sure that there would be no vote on California statehood until after the Texas issue was resolved. Indeed, four days after the Texas boundary vote, the Senate voted 34 to 18 in favor of California statehood. Two southern Democrats voted for the bill, Sam Houston of Texas and Thomas Hart Benton of Missouri, as did Delaware's two Whig senators. Significantly, no other southern Whigs supported California statehood. Webster and Fillmore had pressured New England Whigs to support the Texas bill, but they were unwilling or unable to get any southern Whig support for California. This underscores the lack of "compromise" in the Compromise of 1850.

On August 15 the Senate voted to organize the New Mexico Territory without a ban on slavery, even though by this time everyone was well aware that a convention in New Mexico had written a constitution that would have made it a free state.

Finally, after passing all the laws allowing slavery in the new territories and then admitting California as a free state, the Senate turned to the District of Columbia slave trade bill and the Fugitive Slave Act. As already noted, the slave trade bill was largely symbolic. It removed an irritation that northerners abhorred, but it had absolutely no effect on the system of slavery or even the sale of slaves. Webster, Stephen A. Douglas, and Fillmore sold this law to northerners as a fair trade-off for the new fugitive slave law. But that was a mirage.

Each bill also had to pass the House, where the politics were more complex. Northerners had a huge majority there and might have blocked some of the pro-slavery measures. The final vote on the New Mexico–Texas boundary was possible only because Fillmore pressured northern Whigs in the House to support the bill even though most had been elected on pledges that they would never vote to allow slavery in the new territories. Most telling, perhaps, was the successful pressure placed on Representative Abraham Schermerhorn of Rochester, which was in the heart of New York's antislavery "Burned-over District" and home of the nation's most famous black abolitionist, Frederick Douglass. As one historian has noted, the congressman "buckled under pressure" because Fillmore was prepared to do everything in his power to block Schermerhorn's renomination.[16] Using threats and promises of patronage, Fillmore managed to get just enough votes in the House to get each component of the compromise through.

In September it all came together. On September 9 Fillmore signed bills on the New Mexico–Texas boundary, California statehood, and the Utah Territory. Slavery was now legal everywhere in the new territories, including land well north of the Missouri Compromise line. This was a huge victory for the South, especially when paired with the settlement over Texas giving that slave state more land and $10 million. Since 1787 every territory where slavery was allowed had become a slave state. While some politicians like Clay, Webster, and Douglas argued that slavery was unsuited for these territories, southerners disagreed. Slaves had historically been used in mining and in ranching. Indeed, the first "cowboys" in America were black slaves in South Carolina. If what had just become west Texas was viable slave country—as the Texans insisted—then so too would be the land just over the border in New Mexico and in the potential mining country of Utah.

On September 18, Fillmore signed the new Fugitive Slave Act. Two days later a last crumb was offered to the North as Fillmore signed the bill prohibiting bringing slaves into the District of Columbia for the purpose of sale. It did not prevent the private sale of slaves already in the District. Nor did it prevent people from moving into the District with slaves. It was a symbolic victory for freedom but nothing more.

The abandonment of both the Wilmot Proviso and the Missouri Compromise would lead to a decade of controversy over the status of slavery in the territories. Emboldened by his success in 1850 with the cooperation of a Whig president, in 1854 Stephen A. Douglas would contrive, with the help of a Democratic president, to eviscerate almost all that remained of the Missouri Compromise line with the passage of the Kansas-Nebraska Act. This law set the stage for "Bleeding Kansas" and the final crisis leading to the Civil War. These long-term consequences of the New Mexico and Utah bills were in the future and not readily apparent during Fillmore's administration. What was apparent, from the moment it was conceived, was the potential disaster that the new Fugitive Slave Act would cause. Fillmore's enthusiastic support for this law, and his aggressive enforcement of it, would become the hallmark of his administration. This, even more than the territorial bills, destroyed Fillmore's administration and, with it, the Whig Party.

. . .

The Fugitive Slave Act of 1850 was one of the most repressive and unfair statutes ever adopted by the United States. It was also a law that created, for the first time, a national system of law enforcement. In the wake of *Prigg v. Pennsylvania*, state officials throughout the North had refused to enforce the Fugitive Slave Act of 1793, and a number of states passed legislation prohibiting their judges from hearing fugitive slave cases and prohibiting federal officials or private slave catchers from using state jails to secure alleged fugitive slaves. Southerners complained, with some legitimacy, that these new personal liberty laws made it impossible for them to exercise their constitutional right to recover fugitive slaves. With only a few federal courts operating in the country and a similarly small number of federal marshals, masters had to pursue their slaves on their own or with professional slave catchers. The 1850 law remedied this situation by providing for the appointment of federal commissioners in every county who were empowered to hear fugitive slave cases and call up sufficient force to implement the law.

Under the law federal marshals could be fined $1,000 if they failed to "use all proper means to diligently" execute the law. Marshals and commissioners were empowered to call on the state militia and the United States Army, and to create a federal posse to enforce the law. The statute gratuitously declared that "all good citizens are hereby commanded to aid and assist in the prompt and efficient execution of this law" although there was no clear remedy if citizens refused to help enforce the law.[17] If these measures failed, however, and marshals were unable to prevent a rescue by a mob, they could be held personally liable for the value of any slave who escaped their custody. No other federal law had ever provided such penalties for officers who were unable to implement a law.

Anyone who aided or harbored a fugitive slave or interfered

with the rendition process, for whatever reason, was subject to a $1,000 fine and six months in jail. In addition, they were subject to civil damages of $1,000 to be paid to the owner of a slave for each slave who was not recovered. Many northerners found these provisions particularly obnoxious because, if literally enforced, a farmer could be fined, sued, or jailed for giving a cup of water to a black person walking down the road. The harsh penalties and the minimal standards of proof could force northern whites to assume that all blacks they saw were fugitives, even though in 1850 there were more than 150,000 free blacks living in the North. The new law not only imperiled the liberty of free blacks but also undermined their relationships with their white neighbors. Even a free black in the North might be reluctant to hire another black for fear the person was a fugitive, and the very act of hiring could be a violation of the law. From the perspective of blacks and many white northerners, the act of 1850 had brought the law of slavery into the free states and required northerners to do the bidding of southerners.

These provisions punished free people—white and black—if they helped fugitives. Even more obnoxious were the procedures for returning a slave. Under the law, the alleged slave would get a summary hearing before a federal judge or commissioner. The court was precluded from even considering a writ of habeas corpus. This was the first time the U.S. Congress had suspended the privilege of the writ of habeas corpus, and it was done in violation of the constitutional provision holding that "The Privilege of the Writ of Habeas Corpus shall not be suspended" except in response to an invasion or rebellion.[18]

The law required that a commissioner or judge "hear and determine the case" in "a summary manner," without a jury. The claimant had only to present "satisfactory proof" that the person claimed was a fugitive slave, and this could be done by "deposition or affidavit, in writing, to be taken and certified" before any judge or magistrate in the home state of the slave owner. The potential for fraud, or even mistaken identity, was huge. A master could send his agent to a city in the North to bring back a slave the agent had never seen before. The agent might seize any black person who fit the description in the "deposition or affidavit," bring the individual before a judge, and demand the right to remove the person as a fugitive slave.

The most outrageous and unfair aspect of the law involved the testimony of the alleged fugitive. According to the law, "In no trial or hearing under this act shall the testimony of such alleged fugitive be admitted in evidence." Under this law someone could be dragged south as a slave and never be allowed to offer his or her own voice as evidence that he or she was free. As one northern minister complained, "It requires but the collusion of two men to seize a freeman in the streets of New York or Boston, to drag him before a commissioner, to make affidavit of his escape from service and of his personal identity, and in one hour the freeman shall be in the custody of an armed force on his way to the slave coffles . . . to be sold to the rice plantations of the South."[19]

The outrageousness of the testimony provision was matched by the offensiveness of the provision for paying the commissioners and judges who heard these cases. If a judge ruled against the claimant, thus setting the alleged slave free, the judge was entitled to a five-dollar fee. If the judge ruled for the master, he got a ten-dollar fee. Most northerners viewed this as a blatant attempt to bribe the courts.

Even if one completely supported the rights of masters to recover fugitive slaves, the law needlessly threatened free blacks and unnecessarily trampled on traditional American notions of due process and the fair administration of justice. It was not a law that could be considered part of a "compromise" because it was so utterly one-sided. In addition to all of the denials of due process and the apparent attempt to buy justice, the law made no provisions to protect free people who might be illegally seized under it. There was no anti-kidnapping provision that would have ameliorated northern sensibilities. A northern white could be fined, jailed, and sued for helping a black person who he mistakenly thought was free, but a southerner would face no sanction for seizing a free black and fraudulently or mistakenly claiming him or her as a slave.

The provision for paying judges illustrates Fillmore's political ineptitude and his utter disregard for basic fairness. Defenders of the law claimed that the differential payment was necessary because it took more time to fill out paperwork if the commissioner held that the person before him was a fugitive slave. This was clearly true, but from a political perspective and a moral perspective this was completely beside the point. The law, as written, appeared to bribe commissioners with a double payment if they found in favor of the slave owner.

The historian Elbert Smith has written that the law would "neither go away nor stop plaguing Fillmore's conscience," asserting that Fillmore "delayed signing the bill as long as he could" and signed it only after receiving a formal opinion on the bill's constitutionality from his slaveholding attorney general, John Crittenden.[20] Similarly the historian Robert Rayback, the author of the only full scholarly biography of Fillmore, wrote that Fillmore found the law "repugnant" and that "he hesitated" in signing it.[21] These claims have been the received wisdom about Fillmore. But this is not in fact what happened.

Throughout the summer Fillmore never once suggested that this bill needed to be altered to guarantee due process. Rather, after Clay's omnibus bill failed, Fillmore was, in the words of Michael F. Holt, the greatest historian of the Whig Party, "adamant about passing . . . the fugitive slave measure."[22] If Fillmore truly had doubts about its constitutionality—if he knew his conscience would be bothered by signing the law—it is surprising that he did not mention these concerns in some communication to Congress. He communicated with Congress over the Texas boundary. He let his allies and friends in Congress know that he opposed New Mexico statehood. He asked Congress to fund lighthouses and build a new mint in San Francisco. He was never shy about requesting legislation. Indeed, as Holt notes, after the omnibus bill failed, Fillmore "intensified his intervention in Congress's proceedings."[23] If he was bothered by the Fugitive Slave Act, or any particular provisions, we have no evidence of it.

Nor is there the slightest evidence that he "hesitated" or "delayed" signing the bill as long as he could." The fugitive slave bill passed in the Senate on August 26, without any input from the president. On September 12, the House passed the bill, still without any input or communication from Fillmore, and sent it back to the Senate. On September 16, the presiding officer of the Senate reported that the bill had been delivered to the president, who signed it two days later. He clearly did not "delay signing the bill" for "as long as possible," although he did let it sit on his desk for more than a day, as he waited for Attorney General Crittenden to formally endorse the bill, which Crittenden did on September 18, the day Fillmore signed it into law.[24]

Did this bill plague Fillmore's conscience? The evidence suggests otherwise. More than a month after its passage, Fillmore told Webster, "The law, having been passed, must be executed." He emphatically asserted that "so far as it provides for the surrender of fugitives from labor it is according to the requirements of the constitution and should be sustained against all attempts at repeal."[25] It is hard to imagine how, as a lawyer, Fillmore could believe that it did not violate a number of the provisions of the main body of the Constitution and the Bill of Rights to deny someone the right to testify in his own defense and to send a person into slavery without a jury trial, a right to appeal to a higher court, and the right to apply for a writ of habeas corpus. Apparently, Fillmore forgot that the Fifth Amendment required that no one be deprived of liberty "without due process of law." Fillmore's letter to Webster was hardly the voice of a man who had any pangs of conscience. He did concede that "if there be any provision in it endangering the liberty of those who are free, it should be so modified as to secure the free blacks from such an abuse of the object of the law, and that done we at the North have no just cause of complaint."[26]

The language here is profoundly important in understanding Fillmore's position. He saw nothing unconstitutional or even arbitrary about a law that did not allow a man to speak in his own defense as to whether he should be dragged away from where he was living to some other state to be claimed as a slave. He did not even see how this might undermine the liberty of the more than 150,000 free blacks in the North, including the nearly 50,000 who lived in his home state. He saw nothing wrong, or even politically unwise, in paying commissioners twice as much money for sending a man to slavery as sending him to freedom. He was willing to concede only that "if" there was a provision that endangered the liberty of free people, he would not object to changing the law. Clearly, Fillmore saw nothing in the statute that was dangerous to liberty. In fact, he would soon reject consideration of any change in the law.

In the next two years Fillmore would expend enormous energy overseeing the enforcement of the Fugitive Slave Act. At no time would he express any doubts about the constitutionality of the law. Nor could he see why some people might think it was dangerous or unfair to free blacks or northern whites. This was consistent with his lifelong obtuseness on slavery and the rights of free blacks.

Privately, Fillmore told Webster, "God knows that I detest Slavery."[27] Perhaps the Almighty did know that Fillmore secretly detested slavery, but no human being would have seen this in his policies, his speeches, or the acts of his administration. He told Webster that slavery was "an existing evil, for which we are not responsible, and we must endure it,"[28] but in fact he more than endured it; he protected it. His notion of compromise was to give everything to slavery and not even blink at the act's fundamental denials of due process in the law, its harshness, or the way it threatened all northerners. From all the available evidence—including the aggressive tactics of his administration—his biographers were clearly wrong about how the law affected Fillmore's conscience. But they were absolutely correct that it would not "go away." Indeed, it would dominate the rest of his administration, taint everything else he did, and in the end help destroy his presidency, his party, and ultimately the Union itself.

5

Manifest Destiny and
a Whig Presidency

The expansion into Mexico had been part of a larger movement generally known as Manifest Destiny. Coined by the journalist John L. O'Sullivan, the phrase provided an ideology—a nationalistic theology really—to justify territorial expansion. In defending the annexation of Texas, O'Sullivan declared that territorial acquisition was "the fulfillment of our manifest destiny to overspread the continent allotted by Providence for the free development of our yearly multiplying millions."[1] Like most public men of this period, Fillmore believed in America's Manifest Destiny, but unlike the Democratic version of this idea, Fillmore's Whig programs did not include territorial expansion. Rather, for Fillmore, Manifest Destiny was economic. The Compromise of 1850 was supposed to settle the conflicts over slavery and western expansion. With the compromise passed, Fillmore, a traditional Whig proponent of economic development, had hopes of expanding America's economy through internal improvements, tariffs, and trade.

On December 2, 1850, in his first annual address to Congress, Fillmore promised a noninterventionist foreign policy and declared that in "domestic policy the Constitution will be my guide." He spoke mostly about foreign policy and the economy. He noted a new treaty with the Kingdom of Hawaii, negotiations with Britain to build a canal across Central America, and the need for constitutionally permissible internal improvements, such as lighthouses and "other facilities and securities for commerce and navigation." He argued for federal funding of Great Lakes canal and harbor improvements that, "although local in construction, would yet be national in its purpose and its benefits." Like any orthodox Whig, he urged Congress to pass a tariff that would not only "replenish the Treasury" but have the "incidental advantage" of "encouraging the industry of our own citizens."[2] He focused on developing these programs and policies over the two years remaining in Taylor's term.

. . .

Congress did not immediately respond to Fillmore's request for Great Lakes lighthouses and harbors. A year later he reminded Congress of the need for these improvements, noting that "the whole Northwest appeals to you for relief."[3] The $2 million waterways bill passed that summer spread money across the nation, funding projects from San Diego to Charleston. More than a quarter of the money went to the Great Lakes and their river systems. New York State received more than a quarter of a million dollars, including appropriations for rebuilding the seawall in Buffalo, building dredging equipment on Lake Erie at Buffalo, and a huge $50,000 appropriation for improvements on the upper Hudson River. Fillmore had castigated Polk for not signing a similar bill, and now, after years of arguing for such a program, he was able to implement it. This was probably the most gratifying bill the president from Buffalo ever signed.[4]

In his first address to Congress, Fillmore also asked Congress to establish a United States mint in California because "the laborers in the mines are compelled to dispose of their gold dust at a large discount." In 1852 Congress alleviated this "unjust tax" on miners, as Fillmore characterized it, with legislation creating a new mint in San Francisco.[5] The expansion of the nation to the Pacific slope led, in 1851, to a dramatic reduction in postage costs to a uniform rate of three cents per letter everywhere but the West Coast and six cents to send mail back and forth to California and Oregon. Previously, a letter to California cost forty cents while the cost of a letter in the rest of the country varied from five to twelve cents. This change in postage rates was consistent with Fillmore's longtime interests in stimulating commerce and communication throughout the nation.

Consistent with commercial development, increased internal communication, and Whig economic policy, Fillmore proposed a transcontinental railroad in his first annual message, although nothing would come of it for a number of years because of sectionalism and slavery. Had the Compromise of 1850 been truly successful and diffused sectional animosities, Fillmore might have been able to initiate the transcontinental railroad. Fillmore also worked with private interests to build a shorter railroad across Mexico but refused to use military force—or even the threat of such force—to help the American investors. This project ultimately went nowhere, as did Fillmore's attempt to sponsor a Central American canal. Fillmore similarly refused to use the military to protect American merchants when a new Peruvian government tried to interfere with their purchase of guano on the Lobos Islands. Rather, Fillmore successfully negotiated a settlement with Peru while providing some compensation to the merchants. Fillmore favored commercial expansion but not at bayonet point.

•   •   •

Fillmore's refusal to use the military to help commercial ventures was consistent with his generally noninterventionist foreign policy. Working with Webster, he deftly averted a crisis with the Hapsburg empire over Hungarian independence and helped negotiate the release from a Turkish jail of the Hungarian patriot Louis Kossuth. When Kossuth came to the United States, Fillmore attempted to meet with the charismatic revolutionary in a quiet setting, hoping to offer his personal support for an independent Hungary but not take any public stand. The shrewder and more politically savvy Kossuth came to the White House and used the occasion to make a dramatic, and public, speech that Fillmore did not want to witness or even hear. Fillmore backed away from any public support of Kossuth, even as Congress lionized him. Fillmore might have gained substantial political support for himself, his presidency, and the Whig Party by openly embracing the popular Kossuth, but such a position cut against Fillmore's personality and his views on internationalism.

Fillmore's support for a proposed treaty with Switzerland illustrates his passivity and his general desire to avoid conflict in international relations while at the same time encouraging commercial expansion—economic manifest destiny—at any cost. His support for the treaty also underscores his lifelong flirtations with nativism and his disregard for minorities. The Swiss treaty purported to allow citizens of both nations to travel to and conduct business in either country but guaranteed such rights only for Christian Americans. The Swiss cantons had enormous autonomy in governing the status of people in their jurisdictions, just as the American states did. A number of the cantons extended equal privileges to "Christians alone" and prohibited Jews from conducting business in, or even visiting, their jurisdictions. Secretary of State Webster, speaking for the administration, saw "nothing to object to" in the agreement and submitted the treaty for ratification.[6] For Fillmore and Webster, the concerns of Jews were insignificant.

Though few in number, American Jews vigorously protested against this treaty because it denied them the same rights abroad as Christian Americans. A few Whigs, including Henry Clay and John McPherson Berrien, protested the treaty on the floor of the Senate. Under pressure, Webster and Fillmore backed off, and the president told the Senate he could not endorse a treaty under such circumstances. In 1853, just a month before he left office, the lame-duck Fillmore submitted a new treaty to the Senate with watered-down language, written by the Swiss, that still did nothing to ensure the rights of American Jews. The new treaty language said that American and Swiss citizens would be "admitted and treated upon a footing of reciprocal equality in the two countries, where such admission and treatment shall not conflict with the constitutional and legal provisions, as well Federal as State and Cantonal of the contracting parties." Fillmore asserted that this "modification" allowed him to support the treaty "upon a reasonable principle of compromise."[7] This language of course provided no protection whatsoever for Jews or any other Americans that the Swiss deemed not to be "Christians."

Fillmore's initial support for the Swiss treaty and his subsequent willingness to bargain away the rights of Jewish Americans mirrored his willingness to sacrifice the rights of northern free blacks in the Fugitive Slave Act of 1850. Like the Compromise of 1850, Fillmore's Swiss treaty sacrificed the civil liberties and rights of an American minority group on the altar of political expediency and economic development. The new language was clearly a subterfuge, since it allowed the cantons to exclude, expel, or even arrest Jewish Americans. Fillmore's support for this treaty was also consistent with his long connections to nativism and his hostility to Catholics and immigrants.[8]

Fillmore's most important foreign policy initiative was Commodore Matthew C. Perry's expedition to Japan. Fillmore's interest in Japan was complicated. He had a lifelong fascination with foreign places and cultures; probably his only happy moments as vice president had been in his role as a regent of the Smithsonian Institution. In 1846 he helped gain a charter for the University of Buffalo and became its first chancellor, and he retained that largely honorific position until he died, never stepping down even while he was the comptroller of New York, vice president, and president. Fillmore's personal love of learning was clear. He (or perhaps Abigail, the evidence is unclear) started the White House library, and Fillmore and his family were personally involved in ordering books.[9] Always interested in books, maps, geography, foreign places, and expanding his knowledge, Fillmore took a strong personal interest in Perry's mission to Japan.

Perry's mission to the Chrysanthemum Kingdom had other, more tangible goals. At the time, Japan had virtually closed its ports to the outside world. Shipwrecked European and American sailors who reached Japan were considered criminals and were often horribly mistreated. Protecting sailors was a concern that had popular appeal. Also, many businessmen believed opening Japan to American trade would provide a huge market for American goods. *DeBow's Review* extravagantly predicted that it would quickly reach $200 million a year. America's widening trade with China, extensive whaling industry, and growing Pacific fleet was increasingly based on steamers, and Japan could serve as an ideal coaling station. Finally, an American presence in Japan would be an important counterbalance to Russian, French, and British influence in the Pacific.

Fillmore played a key role in the expedition, writing a letter to the emperor and encouraging Perry in his preparations. In addition to Fillmore's diplomatic and modest letter, carefully wrapped and exquisitely boxed for presentation, Perry brought an eclectic collection of American products designed to awe and impress the Japanese: a small railroad train, a telegraph, farm machinery, a daguerreotype camera, Colt revolvers, Hall rifles, elephant folio sets of John James Audubon's *Birds of America* and *Quadrupeds of North America*, and one hundred gallons of Kentucky bourbon.[10]

Fillmore began planning the expedition to Japan in December 1850. But the project was fraught with delays. His first choice for command proved unfit for the mission, and Fillmore luckily chose Perry to lead the expedition. Congress did not appropriate enough money to pay for all the objects Perry wanted to bring, so he had to spend time getting them gratis. Samuel Colt, understanding the value of international arms sales, volunteered to supply pistols, but Perry had to ask Samuel F. B. Morse for a telegraph machine and then have Morse supply someone to train his sailors to use it. In late November 1852 Perry finally left Norfolk with six ships filled with coal, provisions, presents, and Fillmore's letter to the emperor. The Japan expedition was one of Fillmore's most valuable contributions to American society. He had the vision, or simply the interest in the exotic, to send Perry on his mission. Ironically, and perhaps fittingly for the generally unsuccessful nature of Fillmore's presidency, Perry did not arrive in Japan until July 1853, after Fillmore had left office. Thus, whatever glory came from this farsighted mission went to Fillmore's successor. Perry returned to Japan again in 1854 to sign the Treaty of Kanagawa, which established diplomatic and trade relations between the two countries. It was a major foreign policy success for the Democrat Franklin Pierce, not the Whig Millard Fillmore.

While planning the expedition to Japan probably delighted Fillmore, an expedition to Cuba, which he did not plan, caused him enormous problems and illustrated many of the weaknesses of his administration.

In the aftermath of the war with Mexico, some Americans hungered for yet more land. As noted above, Fillmore resisted military intervention in Peru and Mexico but used diplomacy to solve some problems. Similarly, the president refused to annex Hawaii, although that might have been accomplished. At the same time, however, he forced Napoleon III to back down, in 1851, when he tried to make the Hawaiian Islands a French protectorate. Fillmore imagined that someday Hawaii might become an American territory, but at the moment he wanted an independent Hawaii open to American whalers and traders. Toward that end, he was prepared, if necessary, to protect the kingdom's independence. His firm position was enough to get the French government to back away from interfering in Hawaii's sovereignty.

The most dramatic issue of foreign policy and American Manifest Destiny concerned Cuba. For a number of years, southern adventurers, known as filibusters,[11] had been advocating an American takeover of Cuba, as well as Nicaragua and other parts of Central America. Support for such expeditions came from extreme southern expansionists, who wanted more land for slavery, as well as access to the large number of slaves in Cuba. Senator Albert Gallatin Brown of Mississippi explained why he favored a Caribbean land grab and a future seizure of more of Mexico: "I want Cuba . . . Tamaulipas, Potosi, and one or two other Mexican States; and I want them all for the same reason—for the planting and spreading of slavery."[12]

The most important of these adventurers was Narciso López, a

Venezuelan, who had twice during Taylor's presidency sailed out of New Orleans to invade Cuba. The first time Taylor used the navy to stop López. The second time, in May 1850, López successfully left the port with the connivance of local officials and the help of Governor John A. Quitman of Mississippi. López seized a small town in Cuba before the Spanish army forced him to withdraw. The Taylor administration quickly secured indictments of a number of the leaders, including Governor Quitman. However, the prosecutions did not begin until late 1850, when Fillmore was in office. When the trials of the first two defendants ended in hung juries, the administration dropped all charges against everyone else, including Quitman.

Like Taylor, Fillmore opposed filibustering expeditions, in part because they violated American and international law and could drag the nation into a war. This was also consistent with Whig ideology that opposed using force to increase the nation's size. In April 1851 Fillmore issued an official proclamation condemning filibustering expeditions as "wicked schemes." He warned that any private invasions of Cuba would be regarded as "adventures for plunder and robbery," which would "meet the condemnation of the civilized world." He made it clear that freebooters invading another country would "subject themselves to heavy penalties" of up to $3,000 in fines and three years in prison, and would "forfeit their claim to the protection of this Government."[13]

Fillmore's proclamation was in response to López's activities, as the president knew that López was in New Orleans preparing for another invasion of Cuba. But, despite this knowledge, Fillmore failed to take any serious steps to stop López as he openly recruited soldiers, gathered supplies, and obtained a ship. On August 3 López brazenly sailed out of New Orleans headed for Cuba with four hundred men, including William Crittenden, the nephew of Fillmore's attorney general, who styled himself a colonel in López's army. Fillmore was clearly capable of organizing a major naval expedition to Japan, but he was apparently unable to stop a small ship sailing from an American port to make war on another country.

While Fillmore failed to stop the invasion on the American side, despite the very public nature of López's activities, the Spanish were prepared when it landed. Spanish troops killed about half the invaders and captured the rest. They publicly garroted López in Havana, executed fifty Americans, including Crittenden, by firing squad, and sent 160 prisoners to Spain. News of the executions led to riots in New Orleans, including an attack on the offices of the Spanish consul, who fled the city. Fillmore made no attempts to stop these riots or prosecute the rioters, even though an attack on a diplomat put the crimes within the jurisdiction of the federal government.

When trying to discourage López, Fillmore had boldly proclaimed that these freebooters would "forfeit their claim to the protection of this Government," and would be punished for their "adventures for plunder and robbery." But this is not what happened. Instead, after the López expedition failed, Fillmore negotiated the release from Spain of the captured filibusters. In February 1852, Congress appropriated $6,000 to bring them back to the United States, and Fillmore signed the bill. In July, at Fillmore's request, Congress appropriated an additional $1,000 to pay for the passage to the United States of fifteen foreigners who had been part of the López expedition and were captured and brought to Spain along with their American comrades.[14]

After bringing the men back to the United States, the administration took no steps to prosecute any of them or their financial backers, despite their obvious and brazen violation of American law and their clear threat to American foreign policy. Nor did the administration take any steps against those who rioted and attacked the property of the government of Spain. Fillmore's lackadaisical responses stand in marked contrast to his aggressive use of military force and persistent federal prosecutions against people who interfered with, or merely refused to support, the return of fugitive slaves. While a couple of hung juries discouraged the president from prosecuting the filibusters who had been indicted under the Taylor administration, Fillmore would have a very different response when seeking convictions of opponents of the Fugitive Slave Act.

6

<hr>

A Compromised Presidency

In the wake of the Compromise of 1850, Fillmore surely felt confident. Before the compromise, hotheaded southern extremists were talking disunion, but their attempt at generating support for this movement failed miserably at the Nashville Convention in June. Texans were threatening to go to war against the United States over the sands of New Mexico, although in reality (as Taylor had known) this saber rattling was more like a European comic opera than the tragedy of civil war. Northerners had not threatened the union but made it clear they might punish politicians who allowed slavery into the new territories. And Congress had been paralyzed for at least two sessions.

But the passage of the compromise seemed to have changed all this. Fillmore's major biographer glowingly concludes, "As if by magic, the clouds of disunion, which hovered threateningly over the nation, disappeared. In ten short weeks, Fillmore's administration had solved the problem of territorial government that had plagued Congress ever since American and Mexican troops first clashed four years ago—a problem that had sacrificed all else to its devouring demand for attention."[1] This analysis doubtless reflects how Fillmore felt.

But it wasn't that simple, and the euphoria was short lived.

There was in reality no magic in the compromise, and in the short run—and the long run—the compromise was not very successful. The issue of slavery in the territories had been temporarily settled, but it would reemerge later in the decade; the fugitive slave question would not go away; and barely a decade after Fillmore signed the compromise measure, civil war would break out.

In the short run—that is, Fillmore's remaining time in office—the territorial question would remain quiet, but it would be superseded by an even more divisive issue: the return of fugitive slaves. The new Fugitive Slave Act was a key component of the Compromise of 1850, but there was nothing about the act itself that resembled a compromise. On the contrary, the law was a total appeasement of the most extreme southerners. As noted in chapter 4, the law lacked any semblance of due process and was in fact embarrassingly arbitrary and unfair. Its passage stimulated an enormous backlash.

Fillmore never understood the deep hatred that northerners had for the return of fugitive slaves. When he ran for vice president in 1848, some southerners had suggested that the New Yorker was not safe on the issue of slavery. One southerner claimed he had "countenanced the getting of greasy negroes to Canada." Fillmore's response is fascinating. He told his friend and adviser Nathan K. Hall that this charge was "too infamous to justify a denial," and that he would "as soon think of denying the charge of robbing a hen roost."[2] Fillmore's outrage illustrates not only his conservative doughface politics but also his utter lack of sympathy for runaway slaves. Antislavery Whigs such as William H. Seward or Thaddeus Stevens, as well as the antislavery Democrat Salmon P. Chase, defended men charged with helping fugitive slaves, and even if they would not personally have aided runaways, at one level they "countenanced" such activities. While Fillmore told Webster that he hated slavery—"God knows I detest Slavery"[3]—he had no sympathy for the slave, for free blacks, or for northern whites who *did* have sympathy for the slave.

Although he never fully grasped their motivations, Fillmore understood that the abolitionists would denounce him. But the abolitionists—members of dedicated antislavery organizations—were few in number. Most northerners had never attended a meeting of William Lloyd Garrison's American Anti-Slavery Society or any other national, state, or local organization. Fewer still joined these groups. Even the Liberty Party, which was the only abolitionist political party to field a national candidate, won only 62,300 votes in 1844, out of more than 2.7 million cast. In 1848, the year Fillmore won the vice presidency, Gerrit Smith, running as the National Liberty Party candidate, won a pathetic 2,733 votes. It is true that Martin Van Buren, running as a Free Soiler, won 291,000 votes, but that party was not abolitionist. While some Free Soilers were antislavery radicals, most were more moderate in their opposition to slavery.

The threat to Fillmore's administration did not come merely from abolitionists who opposed slave hunting, but from two other sources: blacks—free and fugitive—living in the North and northern whites not affiliated with the abolitionist movement who were radicalized by the new law. Fillmore, perhaps accepting the racial ideology of the age that blacks were passive and inferior to whites, never anticipated that fugitive slaves would resist slave catchers and that free blacks would come to their aid. Nor could Fillmore and his advisers comprehend that large numbers of whites, who were otherwise not abolitionists or antislavery activists, would be so repelled by the utter unfairness of the law that they too would help alleged fugitives resist reenslavement.

Northern blacks understood that the law threatened their own liberty as well as that of their fugitive slave neighbors. Some blacks, both free and fugitive, fled to Canada or England after the law was passed. Indeed, the administration was embarrassed shortly after the law was passed when two famous fugitives in Boston, William and Ellen Craft, were able to sail to England before the U.S. marshal could seize them. Typical of black responses to the law was an Ohio clergyman who wondered, "Would not the Devil do well to *rent out hell* and move to the United States, and rival, if possible, President Fillmore and his political followers?"[4] Throughout the North, blacks, with some white allies, organized for self-protection with plans to ring bells, blow horns, and in other ways notify people that a black person had been seized as a fugitive. In Springfield, Massachusetts, John Brown, who in 1859 would attack the United States armory at Harpers Ferry, organized the League of Gileadites, consisting of armed blacks who, Brown hoped, would make "clean work" of any slave catchers found in their city.[5]

Most of the 150,000 or so African Americans living in the North were not fugitive slaves, but fugitives did live within their communities. Most fugitives were not recent arrivals from the South being hotly pursued by a master. Rather, the majority of them had been in the North for some time, often more than a decade. These fugitives had jobs, some owned property, and many had married in the North. They were parents, spouses, and neighbors of free blacks, and employees and tenants of both blacks and whites. An aggressive search for runaways would disrupt families and communities. For example, the first person returned under the law, James Hamlet, had lived in New York City for a number of years, was married to a free woman from New York, and was the father of free children born in that state. In addition, the lax standards of the 1850 law threatened free people. In Indiana three blacks who looked white were seized by slave catchers from Kentucky. They tried to tell the federal judge that they were not slaves but, of course, under the 1850 law they were not allowed to speak at the hearing. Eventually, they were able to return to Indiana.[6] Both cases illustrated the danger of the law to free blacks, including those married to fugitive slaves or the freeborn children of fugitive slaves. Northern free blacks feared they would be legally "kidnapped" under the law because of its vague evidentiary requirements, the inability of an alleged fugitive even to speak at a hearing, the summary nature of the process, and the fact that commissioners would be paid twice as much if they found in favor of the master than if they found for the alleged slave.

Free blacks and fugitive slaves were not the only northerners who openly opposed the law. For example, the Chicago City Council passed a resolution declaring the law null and void. Fillmore blamed such challenges to his authority on radical abolitionists. But the Chicago City Council was hardly a den of radicalism. In Boston, a meeting chaired by Charles Francis Adams—the son of one president, the grandson of another, and a future U.S. ambassador to Great Britain (under Lincoln)—resolved that the law violated the Constitution, the Declaration of Independence, and "the golden rule of Christianity."[7]

For most northerners slavery was an abstraction, something debated in Congress or denounced by abolitionists. Most northerners rarely even encountered a free black person much less a slave. But the capture of a fugitive galvanized communities and led to public opposition and sometimes violence. Most fugitive slave cases went smoothly though, or smoothly enough. While Fillmore was president, more than one hundred fugitives would be successfully returned to the South, while a few others would be captured and emancipated after local communities raised money to free them.[8]

However, a handful of dramatic cases undermined the law and ultimately Fillmore's presidency. Incidents in Boston, Syracuse, and rural Pennsylvania illustrate the diversity of opposition to the law. These events, along with resistance organized by blacks and their white friends throughout the North, horrified Fillmore, who saw them as a violation of the fundamental principles of the Constitution. He told Webster, "I mean at every sacrifice and at every hazard to perform my duty." He grandly declared that "nullification can not and will not be tolerated."[9] But from the perspective of American blacks and many whites, it was absurd to believe that a person who escaped from bondage should peacefully return to slavery. If this was a "nullification" of the Constitution, it was nevertheless an implementation of the Declaration of Independence. While Fillmore insisted he would enforce the law at all costs, Frederick Douglass suggested that the best way to deal with the new law was "to make a dozen or more dead kidnappers."[10]

The ink was hardly dry on Fillmore's signature when the new fugitive slave law began to undercut the compromise and destabilize Fillmore's presidency. For the next two years he would be obsessed with enforcing the law, just as fugitive slaves were intent on preserving their liberty and their black and white allies were courageously persistent in trying to achieve justice in the "land of the free and the home of the brave."

In New York, the fugitive slave James Hamlet was successfully returned on September 28, 1850, just ten days after the law went into effect. Hamlet was secretly brought before the clerk for the U.S. District Court and whisked away from the city so quickly that his freeborn wife and two freeborn children had no "knowledge of his doom till he was gone" and were "deprived even the mournful consolation of bidding farewell to their husband and father." The American and Foreign Anti-Slavery Society reported the case in a pamphlet and helped raise $800 to purchase Hamlet's freedom. Fillmore must have had some gratification that the new law was so quickly and successfully enforced in his home state but, at the same time, the administration could not have been very pleased when four to five thousand people assembled to greet Hamlet on his return to freedom and denounce the tyrannical law.[11]

Within weeks of Hamlet's rendition, the news was not so good for Fillmore. In Pennsylvania a federal marshal met with resistance, and local citizens refused to serve in a posse, leading to the escape of a slave. Fillmore was livid at this "nullification."[12] Oddly, he did not see the difference between popular resistance to the law and nullification, which had always been understood as a state action. His response also contrasts sharply to the invasion of the New Mexico Territory by armed Texans authorized by the governor of that state. These were acts of nullification, if not treason, as Texans armed themselves to make war on the United States. Fillmore had declared that these armed Texans were just "trespassers" and were to "be regarded merely as intruders."[13] However, when individual citizens simply refused to participate in the enforcement of a federal law, he elevated their passive actions, which might have been unpatriotic but were not technically illegal, to nullification, which was only one step away from secession and treason.

Fillmore soon discovered that the new law provided no mechanism for incarcerating fugitive slaves. Unlike the 1793 law that it replaced, the 1850 law precluded state participation in the rendition process. Fillmore now faced the problem that in Massachusetts and other places federal officials were not allowed to use local jails to incarcerate fugitive slaves. The president fumed that this too was nullification. But, again, it was not. Fillmore, Webster, and Attorney General Crittenden knew that under the Supreme Court's decision in *Prigg v. Pennsylvania* the states were not required to use their resources to enforce the Constitution's Fugitive Slave Clause. The decision also prohibited the states from protecting the freedom of free blacks or fugitives living in their communities. The 1850 law, following the Supreme Court's ruling, put the entire process into the hands of the federal government. Thus, the states could not be accused of nullification for refusing to participate in a process when the law did not require them to do so or even authorize them to do so. Southerners might complain that the North was not cooperative, and Fillmore might bluster that "nullification can not and will not be tolerated." In fact, there was no nullification. Southerners had written the Fugitive Slave Act of 1850 to prevent the states from interfering in the rendition process by entirely federalizing it. Fillmore had signed this law. They were now stuck with it.

. . .

For the rest of his term, Fillmore worked to implement the Fugitive Slave Act. He authorized the use of federal troops, where necessary, to confront opponents of the law. In Philadelphia he made certain that United States Marines stationed at the Philadelphia Navy Yard would be available whenever U.S. marshals, federal judges, or United States commissioners asked for them. He sent new troops to Boston to cow opponents of the law there. Initially, this seemed to work. Some free blacks and fugitive slaves fled to Canada or England, both of which, from the perspective of African Americans, were a "sweet land of liberty." While many northerners continued to denounce the law, it was, for the most part, enforced.

While using an increasing level of force to implement the new

law, Fillmore devoted a great deal of energy to preventing an antislavery revolt in the New York Whig Party. He aggressively used
patronage and threats of political retaliation to ensure both unity
and support for the Compromise of 1850. Many New York Whigs
believed that the new Fugitive Slave Act threatened the liberty of
the fifty thousand free blacks in the state. In New York and else-
where in the North there were Whigs, like Seward, who wanted to
modify the new law to protect free blacks. Fillmore vigorously
opposed this. He would not even consider amending the law.
Statesmanlike leadership might have led to new legislation that
would have been a real compromise. Some states might have coop-
erated with the enforcement of the law if amendments provided
due process for free blacks and perhaps some protection for fugitives who had been living in the North for a long period of time,
had married into the community, and had families. But Fillmore
stubbornly opposed any modifications of the law. Instead, he
wanted the northern states to go beyond the law and offer their
facilities to help with its enforcement. In the short run this strategy
was successful. In New York, Fillmore's allies mostly defeated the
Seward-Weed antislavery wing of the party in the aftermath of the
compromise. In 1850 Whigs retained the New York governorship
and the party remained nominally united behind Fillmore.

While Fillmore focused much of his attention on New York
politics—he was never quite able to rise above state politics—he
also worried about anticompromise sentiment in the South. In
June 1850 extremist southerners, egged on the previous year by
John C. Calhoun, had organized a convention in Nashville to consider secession if the Wilmot Proviso passed. The convention was a
disaster for the secessionists—half of the slave states sent no delegates, and none of the elected Whigs showed up. The best the fire-
eaters could do was to call for another convention to meet *after*
Congress was no longer in session. But Congress stayed in session
all summer and into the fall, finally adjourning in late September
after the compromise measures had been passed. It was, at that
point, the longest congressional session in the nation's history. In

November the southern rights convention reconvened in Nashville, but only seven states were represented and many of the fifty-nine delegates were unelected, self-appointed, would-be secessionists. The compromise had severely undermined their cause, while Calhoun's death in March 1850 had left them without their most important leader. That same month Governor George Towns of Georgia had scheduled an election to choose delegates for a state secession convention. But a coalition led by Howell Cobb and Alexander Stephens won a smashing victory, beating secessionists almost 2 to 1 in the popular vote and electing a convention that had 240 opponents of secession and only 23 supporters. Instead of advocating secession, as Governor Towns hoped, the convention celebrated the Union. The compromise had something to do with this, but so too did high cotton prices and "widespread prosperity." As one historian noted, "There was too much contentment for a secession movement to take root."[14]

On December 2, in the wake of this overwhelming victory in Georgia and the pathetic turnout in Nashville, Fillmore gave his first annual address to Congress. He promised that in "domestic policy the Constitution will be my guide."[15] Although most of his energies up to this time had been spent on the compromise, he devoted the greater part of his address to economic and foreign policy. The compromise came up at the very beginning of the address and again at the end. First he affirmed that he would enforce the compromise and obliquely attacked those who opposed it.

> It must be borne in mind that the country is extensive; that there may be local interests or prejudices rendering a law odious in one part which is not so in another, and that the thoughtless and inconsiderate, misled by their passions or their imaginations, may be induced madly to resist such laws as they disapprove. Such persons should recollect that without law there can be no real practical liberty; that when law is trampled under foot tyranny rules, whether it appears in the form of a military despotism or of popular violence. The law

is the only sure protection of the weak and the only efficient restraint upon the strong. When impartially and faithfully administered, none is beneath its protection and none above its control. You, gentlemen, and the country may be assured that to the utmost of my ability and to the extent of the power vested in me I shall at all times and in all places take care that the laws be faithfully executed. In the discharge of this duty, solemnly imposed upon me by the Constitution and by my oath of office, I shall shrink from no responsibility, and shall endeavor to meet events as they may arise with firmness, as well as with prudence and discretion.[16]

Fillmore concluded with a plea for sectional harmony to allow the compromise to work. He acknowledged that the compromise could not be "received with immediate approbation by people and States" because, he believed, so many Americans had been "prejudiced and heated by the controversies of their representatives." He told the nation that the compromise measures "were necessary to allay asperities and animosities that were rapidly alienating one section of the country from another and destroying those fraternal sentiments which are the strongest supports of the Constitution." He proclaimed the measures were "a settlement in principle and substance—a final settlement of the dangerous and exciting subjects which they embraced" and that the legislation was "final and irrevocable." He predicted that "a great majority of our fellow-citizens sympathize in that spirit and that purpose, and in the main approve and are prepared in all respects to sustain these enactments. I can not doubt that the American people, bound together by kindred blood and common traditions, still cherish a paramount regard for the Union of their fathers, and that they are ready to rebuke any attempt to violate its integrity, to disturb the compromises on which it is based, or to resist the laws which have been enacted under its authority."[17]

Fillmore's spin was predictable. The speech did not directly single out any group, northern or southern, cast blame on any particular individuals, or even mention the Fugitive Slave Act directly. Rather, Fillmore blamed the disharmony on the highly charged rhetoric of politicians. Fillmore condemned those who might resist the law but of course never noted the fundamental due process problems with the law or that it involved taking liberty from people who had escaped the bondage they were born into or took liberty from people who were born free. With no sense of irony, he warned that such lawlessness would undermine all liberty because "without law there can be no real practical liberty" and that this would lead to tyranny "in the form of military despotism or of popular violence."[18]

The neutrality of the speech was truly a facade, because Fillmore's focus, and his anger, was on northerners who opposed the return of fugitive slaves. He publicly reaffirmed that he would take a tough stand on such challenges. In doing so, he missed the irony of his own rhetoric. What, a free black married to a fugitive slave might have asked, was the "real practical liberty" of a law that could drag people back to slavery years, or even decades, after they had found their own liberty in the North, where they married, had children, and bought property? How, many asked, was the Fugitive Slave Act the "sure protection of the weak and the only efficient restraint upon the strong" when blacks, who were the politically and economically weakest in society, were prohibited from even testifying in hearings over their own liberty? Many northerners, black and white, must have wondered how Fillmore could, with a straight face, extol the idea that the law protected people from "military despotism" when he was busy authorizing the use of marines in Philadelphia to ship people to slavery and hurriedly sending troops to Boston to guarantee that fugitives would be dragged back to their masters. Many northerners, black and white, reasonably wondered why Fillmore believed that "none is beneath its [the law's] protection and none above its control" when in fact the Fugitive Slave Act denied any semblance of due process to blacks seized under the law but provided no penalties to slave catchers who seized and attempted to enslave free people.

Fillmore's great fear, of course, was not the fact that the Fugitive

Slave Act was pushing northerners, even conservative Whigs, to oppose his administration and the federal government. He not only did not worry about this, he seemed utterly oblivious to the problem, as he remained unalterably opposed to any modification of the law. This was in part because Fillmore was utterly unconcerned about the fate of free blacks and had long harbored a distaste, if not an actual hatred, of abolitionists. He was concerned, however, that his New York rivals, Seward and Weed, would use the Fugitive Slave Act to undermine support for him in his home state. What he could not see, or comprehend, was that many citizens of New York, including the nearly fifty thousand free blacks who lived there, believed that the law threatened liberty in the North and that it was deeply immoral.

Fillmore also feared offending the South. His southern policy was in part personal, in part partisan, and in part patriotic. The personal had to do with the 1852 election. Since the founding, there had been only three northern-born presidents—John Adams, John Quincy Adams, and Martin Van Buren—and each had held the office for only one term. Harrison, the only other Whig besides Taylor to win a presidential election, lived in Ohio when he was elected, but he came from a patrician Virginia family and had held slaves even while a governor in the Northwest Territory. Furthermore, every successful presidential candidate in the past had won close to half (or more) of the slave states. For Fillmore to win a presidential term on his own—his personal goal—he had to carry a substantial number of southern states. This meant he had to make sure that southerners viewed him as safe on slavery and southern rights. Thus, he had not challenged the Texans—or insinuated that their actions were treason—when they confronted the U.S. Army in New Mexico and tried to take over the government there. But he was willing to arrest and even prosecute for treason northerners who opposed snatching blacks in the free states. The one-sided nature of his policies became even clearer in 1851, when his administration failed to prosecute the filibusters who were obviously breaking federal law by invading Cuba while aggressively prosecuting opponents of the Fugitive Slave Act, including some people who did nothing more than refuse to join a federal posse or who simply denounced the law.

The partisan issue was tied to the 1852 campaign and to Whig Party politics. To have a successful presidency and to win in 1852, Fillmore needed the support of southern Whigs. This meant holding together a party that was truly competitive in only three Deep South states: Georgia, Louisiana, and Florida. A Fillmore victory in 1852 would require carrying one or more of those states, as well as some states in the upper South. In heading off the secessionist movement that led to the two Nashville conventions, Whigs had allied with unionist Democrats, and there was talk of creating a southern unionist party that would absorb the Whigs. This would hurt Fillmore in 1852 and hurt the Whigs in Congress even if he won the election. He hoped to head off this unionist movement by showing that a northern Whig could be a good and reliable ally of slavery.

The patriotic issue is more complex. Fillmore clearly feared a secessionist movement in the South, although many modern historians doubt this was plausible in 1850. Still, the issue is not whether it was plausible but whether Fillmore thought it was plausible. During the compromise debates, Calhoun and other extreme southerners had argued for nullification or secession if the South did not get what it needed out of the legislation. Most southerners saw this movement not as a genuine reflection of prevailing southern sentiments but as a power grab by Democrats who hoped to outflank the Whigs on the compromise and obliterate them in state elections. The strategy failed in both Nashville conventions and in Georgia, where the Whigs, allied with unionist Democrats, utterly demolished the secessionist plans of Governor Towns in the November election. If Fillmore feared secession in December 1850, he was clearly not reading the election results from the Deep South or looking at the complete failure of the Nashville secessionist conventions.

The compromise significantly undermined disunionist sentiments because it was a huge victory for the South. It had destroyed the Wilmot Proviso, eviscerated the Missouri Compromise line, and created a new federal bureaucracy for recovering fugitive slaves. The only concrete gain for the North was California statehood, and all but the most fanatical pro-slavery southerners saw a free California as inevitable. Georgia's Robert Toombs, who was hardly soft on slavery, voted against California statehood but publicly acknowledged that he did "not consider the admission of California an aggression upon the South."[19] Nor did most other southerners. They may have opposed admitting California without a slave state to pair it with, but they surely remembered that Texas and Florida had been admitted without any corresponding free states. With Utah and New Mexico now open to slavery, and Texas larger than ever, the South had room to grow.

The most extreme southern sectionalists were not satisfied, and even after getting soundly drubbed in Georgia and looking utterly foolish at the second Nashville convention, the radicals still pushed the secessionist argument. These radicals understood that the compromise threatened their political goals precisely because the South had won so much that most of their neighbors could not take the secessionist goals seriously. If the compromise worked, then the secessionist arguments of men like Robert Barnwell Rhett of South Carolina, William L. Yancey of Alabama, and John A. Quitman of Mississippi would fall on deaf ears. Thus, while southern extremists pushed for disunion conventions in the aftermath of the compromise, the majority of southerners wanted nothing to do with secession. In Georgia the antisecessionists followed up on their November 1851 victory by turning the state's December convention into a celebration of the Union, passing a resolution supporting the Union and the compromise but also noting that the "preservation of our much beloved Union" depended "upon a faithful execution of the *Fugitive Slave Law*."[20] Fillmore read this as an ominous threat that would force him to take a harder line on fugitive slave enforcement. But a shrewder, smarter president might have read the results to see that he now needed to secure northern support for the return of fugitives, and for once offer something to the opponents of slavery. A modified fugitive slave law, with due process and even a statute of limitations on capturing some runaways, might have done the trick. Fillmore might have paired proposals for modifications of the 1850 law with a public works project to build federal jails throughout the country, in order to have a place to incarcerate suspected fugitives without having to rely on the states. This would have been consistent with Fillmore's love of internal improvements and would have demonstrated to the South that the national government was prepared to spend money to help return fugitives. At the same time, Fillmore could have asked for due process protections for alleged fugitives. However, Fillmore remained adamant that there could be no changes to the compromise.

A year later, in the fall of 1851, unionists won major victories in Georgia, Alabama, South Carolina, and Mississippi. In South Carolina a secessionist ticket lost statewide and the leading secessionist, Robert Barnwell Rhett, resigned from the U.S. Senate in disgust. In the Mississippi governor's race, the unionist Whig, Henry S. Foote, defeated the secessionist Democrat, Jefferson Davis, who of course would later become president of the Confederate States of America. In Georgia, Howell Cobb became governor, replacing the secessionist Towns, while the unionist Toombs retained his House seat until he went to the Senate in 1853.

While unionists were ascendant in the South, Fillmore's fugitive slave policy began to undermine his leadership and his presidency. Never understanding that his fellow northerners truly abhorred the idea of forcing people into servitude, especially without any due process, Fillmore faced three major fugitive slave crises in 1851 where his administration failed to return fugitives and was also unsuccessful in its attempts to prosecute their rescuers. In a fourth case, that of Thomas Sims, the fugitive was returned but at an enormous political cost.

. . .

On February 15, 1851, the United States marshal in Boston arrested a fugitive slave, Shadrach Minkins, who had been living in that city for about nine months. This arrest, in the hometown of the abolitionist movement, was designed to show the South how serious Fillmore was about enforcing the 1850 law. Enforcing the Fugitive Slave Act in Boston would also be enormously supportive of Daniel Webster, proving that the law could be enforced in his backyard despite the public hostility to the law and to Webster for his support of it.

Immediately after Shadrach's[21] arrest, three leading antislavery lawyers, Samuel E. Sewall, Ellis Gray Loring, and Charles G. Davis, volunteered to represent him. Other abolitionist lawyers, including Richard Henry Dana Jr. and the black attorney Robert Morris, attended the hearing. Shadrach's lawyers asked for a postponement to prepare their case and U.S. commissioner George Ticknor Curtis granted this request. Davis and the abolitionist Elizur Wright then stood in the courtroom conversing with Shadrach while about thirty blacks crowded outside. When Davis and Wright left the courtroom, the blacks held the doors open, charged in, overpowered the few federal deputies, and rescued Shadrach. He was quickly hidden and then taken to Canada. Two days later federal authorities arrested Davis for the rescue.

Shadrach's arrest was a propaganda play, and the administration badly mishandled it. The U.S. attorney had as much time as he needed to plan for Shadrach's arrest and hearing and could easily have arranged for appropriate security. Instead, he and the Fillmore administration were embarrassed by the quick response of Boston's black community. The administration apparently could not believe that blacks in the city had planned this quick rescue, and so the U.S. attorney arrested Shadrach's white lawyer. This was a clear, and not particularly subtle, message to Boston's legal community that the Fillmore administration was prepared to retaliate against lawyers who represented fugitives, which stands in contrast to the Fillmore administration's refusal to arrest the people who had contributed to the filibustering expeditions of Narciso López in Cuba.

There was, however, no serious evidence linking Davis to the rescue, and six days after the trial began Commissioner Curtis dismissed the charges against him. The trial proved to be a propaganda victory for opponents of the Fugitive Slave Act. Abolitionists wanted to paint the administration as arbitrary and tyrannical. Fillmore, Webster, and their officials in Boston seemed to be working hard to provide evidence to support the abolitionists' claims.

With the charges against Davis dismissed, the administration ordered the arrest of a number of blacks in Boston for participating in the riot, including the community leader Lewis Hayden and a used-clothing dealer named James Scott. On March 1 authorities arrested two more blacks, the businessman John P. Coburn and the lawyer Robert Morris. At the end of the month the grand jury, guided by the U.S. attorney, brought indictments against two whites and five blacks, including Morris and Scott. Throughout this period Webster was in constant contact with Fillmore, urging that a better attorney be added to the prosecution team because he believed the U.S. attorney, a Taylor appointee, was incompetent. Webster personally appealed to Boston's leading conservative Whig lawyers, including Rufus Choate and Benjamin R. Curtis, but the best he could come up with was an obscure lawyer from Salem. Meanwhile, Richard Henry Dana Jr. took the case of the defendants and was joined by U.S. senator John P. Hale of New Hampshire.

In May, James Scott's trial ended in a hung jury. Immediately thereafter, the trial of Lewis Hayden began. Both Scott and Hayden had clearly participated in the rescue, but many of the prosecution's witnesses were weak, some had criminal records, and others were of uncertain veracity. Senator Hale gave a stirring closing argument, and the next day a second hung jury was dismissed. In the filibustering cases, Fillmore had stopped all prosecutions after two successive hung juries, but this was not to be the pattern in Boston.

The prosecution next tried to initiate the trial of the black lawyer Robert Morris. His relationship to the rescue was less clear since he had been inside the courtroom talking to Shadrach when the rescuers charged in. However, government witnesses were ready to place him in the crowd that rescued Shadrach. Morris's trial began just as the term of the district court was ending, so his case was held over until July, when Supreme Court justice Levi Woodbury would be in Boston to preside over the circuit court. Woodbury, a classic northern doughface who vigorously supported the Fugitive Slave Act, was a darling of southern Democrats. Justice Woodbury hoped to run for president as a Democrat in 1852; presiding over the conviction of one of the few black attorneys in the United States might clinch his nomination. However, in July Woodbury was too ill to hold court, and he died in September. In November Woodbury's replacement on the Supreme Court, Justice Benjamin R. Curtis, presided over the trial. The evidence was conflicting, but Morris provided numerous witnesses who demonstrated that he was a law-abiding attorney, and while he may have conversed with the rescuers he was not one of them. The jury acquitted Morris, even though no one on the jury was openly antislavery and all had declared they did not believe the 1850 law was unconstitutional.

After three trials the administration had still not convicted anyone for the rescue, but Fillmore, stubborn as ever, insisted on continuing to find someone to put in jail to avenge the humiliation of the administration. In June 1852 the federal government prosecuted the white abolitionist Elizur Wright. There was no evidence to tie him to the rescue. Indeed, the prosecution's case was so weak that Wright, who had no legal training, foolishly conducted his own defense. The jury was packed with administration supporters, and even with no evidence against him a majority of the jurors voted for conviction, but a few holdouts led to a hung jury. In November 1852 the prosecution retried Wright. This time Wright used Dana and Hale as a defense team, and, with Justice Curtis presiding, they easily won an acquittal. Most observers praised Curtis for his evenhandedness. A Cotton Whig who supported the compromise and the Fugitive Slave Act, Curtis was a smart, conscientious jurist with no political ambitions. Daniel Webster had been more anxious to convict Wright than anyone else involved in the case. Wright was a superb editor and an unflinching opponent of the Fugitive Slave Act, precisely the kind of moderate and shrewd abolitionist that Fillmore and Webster feared. Thus, twice the administration brought him to trial and twice it failed. Ironically, Wright's outright acquittal came shortly after Webster's death.[22] Symbolically, this acquittal signaled the death of the prosecutions over the Shadrach case.

The multiple Shadrach prosecutions came in the context of three other fugitive slave cases: the successful rendition of Thomas Sims from Boston; the failure to seize any slaves in Christiana, Pennsylvania; and the Jerry Rescue in Syracuse.[23] The two failed renditions demonstrated the ineptitude of the Fillmore administration in enforcing the fugitive slave law, while the subsequent prosecutions revealed a vindictive, overreaching administration that lacked any consistent legal principles. Most of all, the prosecutions underscored the administration's utter incompetence in prosecuting those who resisted the law.

Three months after the Shadrach Rescue, the United States marshal in Boston arranged for the arrest of Thomas Sims, who had escaped from Savannah, Georgia, to Boston in February 1851. He was discovered when he sent a letter to his free black wife in Georgia. Federal and city officials prepared carefully for his arrest. The federal courthouse was ringed with anchor chain, and five hundred special deputies (mostly hired for the occasion) were stationed outside the building. City officials were not responsible for the return of a fugitive slave, but the mayor was responsible for maintaining order in Boston.

Like Shadrach, Sims was brought before U.S. commissioner George T. Curtis. Congressman Robert Rantoul and Ellis Gray Loring represented Sims, and after extensive hearings Curtis ordered Sims returned to Georgia. The lawyers for Sims asked for further delay so proof that Sims was actually a free man could arrive from Georgia. But Curtis, ever the Cotton Whig and Fillmore ally, would have none of this. The hearing had already given Sims more due process than the 1850 law required, and the commissioner was not about to set the stage for another rescue. Curtis simply said that Sims would have ample opportunity to prove his freedom once he was returned to Georgia. Under guard of more than one hundred policemen, Sims was marched from the courthouse, placed on a ship, and sent to Georgia, where he received thirty-nine lashes, but no judicial hearing on his status, before being sent to work.

At one level, this was a victory for Fillmore and Webster. The "honor" of Massachusetts had been redeemed by the return of Sims. But the cost was huge. For days Boston was an occupied city. At the time the federal courts in Boston shared a building with the Massachusetts Supreme Judicial Court; in putting three layers of anchor chain—and five hundred policemen—around the federal court, the Fillmore administration had also effectively chained off the Massachusetts courts. The aged and venerable Chief Justice Lemuel Shaw, the most respected state jurist in the nation, was forced to stoop under the chains. No abolitionist in the nation could have designed a better image to excoriate President Fillmore and his minions: the national executive, a native of New York and the son of New Englanders, had chained up justice in the very citadel of the American Revolution. The abolitionists did not like Shaw, but they loved the image. An abolitionist minister wrote Charles Sumner, who would soon become a leader of the abolitionist wing of the Republican Party: "Think of old stiff-necked Lemuel visibly going under the chain! That was a spectacle!"[24] In humiliating one of the most respected judges in America, as well as one of the most revered men in Massachusetts, Fillmore and the "ichabod" Webster probably did more damage to the Fugitive Slave Act than any speeches by abolitionists such as William Lloyd Garrison or Wendell Phillips.

On September 11, 1851, Edward Gorsuch, a Maryland slave owner, and a handful of his relatives and neighbors attempted to seize a fugitive slave near the town of Christiana, in Lancaster County, Pennsylvania. Accompanied by U.S. deputy marshal Henry H. Kline, the Gorsuch party went to the home of a fugitive slave named William Parker, where a number of fugitives (including Gorsuch's) lived. The blacks in Parker's house quickly blew horns and rang bells, and soon many blacks and a few whites, including Castner Hanway and Elijah Lewis, arrived at Parker's house. Kline asked Hanway and the other whites (all of whom were unarmed) to serve in a posse, but they refused and instead urged Kline and Gorsuch to leave before violence occurred. None of the whites present (nor most of the blacks) did anything to stop Gorsuch and Kline, but the presence of a growing number of blacks intimidated the marshal and the other slave catchers. So too did Parker's statement that he was armed and ready to fight to defend his freedom. Realizing he was vastly outnumbered, and probably outgunned, Kline urged Gorsuch to leave, but the Maryland slave owner refused, saying, "I will have my property, or go to hell." He then tried to enter Parker's house. A firefight soon erupted, in which Parker killed Gorsuch; all the other white slave catchers except Kline (who ran from the scene before the fighting) were wounded. All of the blacks in Parker's house successfully fled the area. Parker calmly took a train to Rochester, New York, where he visited Frederick Douglass. Parker gave Douglass the pistol he had used to kill Gorsuch, and the next day he took a boat to Canada.

Three weeks later, in Syracuse, New York, the administration tried to enforce the law again, arresting a fugitive slave named Jerry. This arrest had been planned in Washington. Earlier that spring Webster, while visiting Syracuse, had denounced opponents of the law and had publicly declared: "Depend upon it, the law will be executed in its spirit, and to its letter. It will be executed in all the great cities; here in Syracuse; in the midst of the next Anti-slavery Convention, if the occasion shall arise."[25] The administration now tried to do this.

In October 1851 Syracuse hosted a Liberty Party convention, and the town was also filled with people attending the state agricultural fair, most of whom came from antislavery communities. It is hard to imagine what Fillmore thought would be accomplished by directly challenging opponents of slavery in the heart of central New York, one of the most antislavery regions in the country. Perhaps Fillmore felt he had to prove that the law could be enforced anywhere, or perhaps he was so offended by northern opposition to the law that he was determined to mock its opponents.

Prudence would have dictated arresting Jerry when Syracuse was not filled with abolitionists and antislavery tourists, but Fillmore's stubbornness, his almost fanatical hatred of abolitionists, and his desire to prove what might be described as pro-slavery machismo prevailed. It is hard to imagine purposefully designing a plan that could have been worse. That night a mob of some five thousand people gathered outside the jail, where the U. S. marshal and a few deputies were clearly unable to hold their prisoner. The Jerry Rescue was a major failure of the law of 1851. Jerry ended up in Canada.

Fillmore responded to the Christiana riot and the Jerry Rescue with demands for prosecutions. In Pennsylvania the administration oversaw the indictment for treason of Hanway, Lewis, three other whites, and thirty-six blacks, as Fillmore and Webster personally corresponded with the U.S. attorney John W. Ashmead. The decision to bring treason indictments was made at a meeting that included Fillmore, Webster, Ashmead, and Attorney General Crittenden. Ashmead argued that resistance to the law was not treason, and it was hardly clear that Hanway, who simply declined to join the posse, could even be convicted of resisting the law. But Fillmore wanted a treason prosecution, in part because political operatives in Maryland and the other slave states assured him that this was the way to secure the Whig nomination and the election in 1852. To help ensure a conviction, Fillmore authorized Ashmead to hire two extra lawyers to help him prepare this extensive case.[26]

In November 1851 the administration began what to this day remains the largest treason trial in the entire history of the United States. While this was a federal indictment, by the time the case went to trial Fillmore had allowed four outside attorneys to join the prosecution. Maryland sent Attorney General Robert J. Brent and then hired Senator James Cooper of Pennsylvania to help him. At the last minute the U.S. attorney from Baltimore, Z. Collins Lee, joined the team, not as a federal prosecutor but on a retainer from Maryland. Finally, the Gorsuch family hired the Philadelphia recorder R. M. Lee to help the prosecution. Thus, two private attorneys, a state attorney general, and a U.S. attorney from another jurisdiction, appearing as private counsel, were allowed to join the prosecution. This array of seven lawyers prosecuting a federal treason trial was unique in American history.

The Christiana trials further embarrassed Fillmore even as the effort, however botched, increased his popularity in the South. In November the government brought all the defendants to court, planning to try them one at a time, beginning with Castner Hanway, who had five attorneys, led by Congressman Thaddeus Stevens and John M. Read, a leading Philadelphia Democrat.

Supreme Court justice Robert Grier, a Pennsylvania doughface known to support slavery and oppose abolitionists, presided over the trial, while attending to his circuit duties.[27] The prosecution was divided, and the seven lawyers did not get along. In his opening statement one of Hanway's lawyers mocked the prosecution and the absurd charge of treason: "Did you hear it? Three harmless, nonresisting Quakers and eight and thirty wretched, miserable, penniless negroes, armed with corn-cutters, clubs, and a few muskets, and headed by a miller [the non-Quaker Hanway], in a felt hat, without a coat, without arms, and mounted on a sorrel nag, levied war against the United States. Blessed be God that our Union has survived the shock."[28] The sarcasm was on point. After days of testimony Justice Grier charged the jury that even if Hanway was guilty of something—and the evidence was weak on this point—he was not guilty of treason, which was a "public crime" of making war against the government. He compared the opponents of the law to smugglers who break the law for their own gain, and he noted that "resistance" to "the execution of a law of the United States . . . for a private purpose, is not treason." Grier concluded that "it would be dangerous precedent for the court and jury in this case to extend the crime of treason by construction to doubtful cases, and our decision would probably operate in the end to defeat the purposes of the law, which the government seeks to enforce."[29] This ended the Christiana treason trials.

The administration's use of treason prosecutions—a clear case of prosecutorial overkill—failed miserably. Even a doughface like Justice Grier could not support this misuse of the law. Webster, a great lawyer, surely should have known better. Similarly, President Fillmore was a good enough lawyer to know that whatever had happened in Christiana it was not treason. But Fillmore had been privately claiming that opponents of the law were traitors. His anger and frustration, his utter lack of vision, and his overwhelming desire to please the South led him to personally intervene in the case, over-rule his own U.S. attorney, and push for treason indictments that could not be sustained.

The Syracuse trials hardly went any better for Fillmore than those in Boston and Pennsylvania. Two different grand juries, one in Buffalo and one in Albany, indicted thirteen rescuers. These cities were about 150 miles from Syracuse but both were in the Northern District of New York, and thus in the district where the rescue took place. Holding the trials so far from Syracuse greatly inconvenienced the defendants, once again showing the vindictive nature of the Fillmore administration. Albany and Buffalo were also the most conservative cities in the district, with the greatest support for Fillmore's compromise and the Fugitive Slave Act. The administration hoped the more conservative jurors in these cities would vote for convictions. In addition, Fillmore was from Buffalo, and he had lived in Albany and perhaps hoped this would give the prosecution the legal equivalent of a "home field" advantage. But even in these cities, convictions were difficult. Only one defendant, Enoch Reed, a free black man, was convicted, and he died of natural causes while his case was on appeal. Other cases led to hung juries or were dismissed or simply languished. As late as 1857, the federal courts were still sorting out the indictments. Significantly, when the first group of rescuers were indicted, they were bailed out by another New York state politician: Senator William Henry Seward of Auburn.

The fugitive slave cases stood in stark contrast to Fillmore's handling of the Cuban filibusters. The crimes committed by the filibusters were serious and threatened international relations. But when the trials of two minor players, who had been indicted under Taylor, ended in hung juries, Fillmore dropped all prosecutions and never again tried to prosecute subsequent filibusters. Fillmore later warned filibusters that through their illegal behavior they would "forfeit their claim to the protection of this Government."[30] In the end, however, he not only refused to push for prosecutions but used diplomatic capital and federal funds to bring them back from Spain. While refusing to move against filibusters, he relentlessly pursued prosecutions of northerners who interfered with—or simply opposed—the Fugitive Slave Act. His stubbornness in insisting on such reckless enforcement in the face of antislavery hostility underscores Secretary of the Interior Alexander H. H. Stuart's observations that when Fillmore "had satisfied himself that he was right, no power on earth, could induce him to swerve from what he believed to be the line of duty."[31] Some of those prosecuted for the Shadrach Rescue, such as Elizur Wright, had nothing to do with the rescue, but Fillmore had him retried after a hung jury. In Christiana, Castner Hanway had merely refused to accept an appointment to a federal posse. The 1850 law urged "all good citizens" to join such posses, but it did not require participation and provided no penalty for those, like Hanway, who would not participate. Fillmore found a crime: treason, which of course carried the death penalty.

The 1850 law and Fillmore's reckless enforcement of it would be Fillmore's legacy. His presidency, from the signing of the Compromise of 1850 through the Shadrach and Jerry prosecutions into late 1852, was aggressively pro-slavery. He would be remembered as the first of three doughface presidents in the 1850s. It was a reputation well earned.

7

Defeat, Failed Resurrection, and Retirement

Fillmore's biographers claim he was never interested in running for a full term on his own and agreed to do so in 1852 only when it was clear the Whig Party "needed" him. The evidence for this argument is mixed. His correspondence on enforcing the Fugitive Slave Act has a distinctly political flavor. His direct involvement in the Christiana treason prosecutions and his willingness to allow Maryland to help with the prosecution surely suggests that he was interested in shoring up his political support in that state and the rest of the South for an 1852 run for the presidency. From the White House, he carefully monitored political events and party politics throughout the nation. He discouraged the formation of "union" parties because they might obliterate the Whig Party in the South. He actively engaged in correspondence and conversation with newspaper editors. When newspapers endorsed Fillmore for president, as the *Philadelphia Sun* did in March 1851, he raised no objections and welcomed their support. He urged his allies to buy newspapers, such as the *Albany Register,* and used his influence to choose editors. None of this should be surprising. Nineteenth-century politics was largely carried out in the newspapers, and effective presidents needed partisan newspapers as much as they needed the patronage machine created by appointing postmasters throughout the nation. Fillmore's early appointment of Nathan K. Hall as post-master general was not just a plum for his oldest friend and ally. It was a classic move of putting a trusted confidant in a position to dole out patronage to strengthen his political power.[1]

In December 1851 he informed his friend and confidant Dr. Thomas Foote that he was not going to be a candidate in 1852, but Foote easily convinced the notoriously stubborn Fillmore to post-pone any announcement.[2] Clearly, he was not truly committed to retirement and seemed to be strategically placing himself so he could run.

By this time Secretary of State Daniel Webster had announced his intention to seek the presidency once again, and Fillmore may have privately endorsed his candidacy. Normally, it would be con-sidered utterly unacceptable for a cabinet member to challenge a sitting president for the nomination. Lincoln would remove Secre-tary of the Treasury Salmon P. Chase when he began to explore a run for the 1864 nomination. But Fillmore did nothing to discour-age Webster, which may indicate that he really did not want to run.

However, Fillmore's tolerance of Webster's candidacy may also have been a shrewd and calculated move. Fillmore knew that Web-ster was ill and utterly unfit to run for the office, much less hold it. According to one observer, Webster was now a "poor, decrepit old man, whose limbs could scarcely support him; whose sluggish legs were somewhat concealed by an overhanging abdomen."[3] It seems likely that Fillmore tolerated the aging secretary of state's last hur-rah in part because he could effectively serve as a placeholder for Fillmore himself. In November 1851 Edward Everett of Massachu-setts told Fillmore that he was supporting Webster out of friend-ship and New England solidarity, but when it came to actually choosing a candidate, "I shall hold myself in a position to give cor-dial support to your nomination."[4] Fillmore believed that his real nemesis, after all, was not his increasingly decrepit secretary of state, but his New York rival Senator Seward. Fillmore may have seen a Webster campaign in 1851 as the perfect foil to distract Seward. This strategy, however, would ultimately backfire, like so much else in Fillmore's administration, and would cost him the nomination.

By early 1852 Fillmore was clearly a candidate, with newspapers daily endorsing him and correspondents from all over the nation begging him to run. Fillmore had strong support in the South and among the newest version of nativism, the Know-Nothings. In Philadelphia the leader of this new movement told the president, "The Native Americans are for you to a man."[5] As he had so often, Fillmore embraced this anti-Catholic support. Southern Whigs praised his unyielding enforcement of the Fugitive Slave Act. In the South freedom of expression regarding slavery had long since disappeared, and no whites (nor of course any blacks) could openly oppose slavery or disagree with the wisdom of the Fugitive Slave Act. The 1850 act had brought southern notions of justice and race into the North, and by the end of 1851 Fillmore was becoming increasingly southern in his approach to slavery. The continued prosecution of Elizur Wright and the treason prosecutions in Pennsylvania can be seen as crassly political, just as were Fillmore's refusal to prosecute filibusters. Not surprisingly, southern Whigs were enamored of Fillmore and wanted to see him run for president. Never before had the South had a northern president who was so obsequiously willing to protect slavery.[6]

Meanwhile, northern Whigs were coalescing around General Winfield Scott. He had been born into a rich planter family in Virginia and had married into an even wealthier Richmond family. Scott had practiced law before embarking on a military career that began in 1808. He was a hero of both the War of 1812 and the Mexican War. Scott had been considered for the Whig nomination in 1840 and 1844 and ran second to Taylor at the 1848 Whig Convention. Antislavery Whigs, including Seward, supported him because, like Taylor, he was a moderate on slavery even though he was a southern slaveholder himself. Fillmore feared him, in part, because Seward supported him.

The Whigs met in Baltimore in June 1852. Despite the defeat of southern extremists in 1850 and 1851, Whigs, especially in the

North, had done poorly in the off-year elections. Fillmore had managed to crush most of the internal opposition to the Compromise of 1850 and the Fugitive Slave Act, but the cost was huge. Ambivalent about running on his own, or perhaps insecure, initially he had not effectively used patronage to shore up his support within the party. He sought harmony within the party most of the time, but then at other times bullied opponents of the Fugitive Slave Act with heavy-handed tactics that worked in the short run but alienated his fellow Whigs. The seemingly endless fugitive slave prosecutions in Massachusetts and New York and the absurd treason case in Pennsylvania made Fillmore appear to be vindictive and opportunistic. The Seward wing of the party painted him as a hypocrite who had sold his antislavery credentials for southern support. This was incorrect, but only because Fillmore had *never* really been antislavery, even though in 1848 he had gained the vice presidential nomination because his supporters dishonestly asserted that he favored the Wilmot Proviso. A truer portrayal of Fillmore would hardly have been more flattering: he had emerged as the most doughface politician in the nation. He stubbornly refused to consider any changes to the Fugitive Slave Act despite its grotesquely unfair provisions, and he went after those who opposed the law with the fanaticism of a grand inquisitor.

Both political conventions in 1852 were dysfunctional and confused. The Democrats took forty-nine ballots to nominate the virtually unknown Franklin Pierce of New Hampshire, after Lewis Cass, James Buchanan, and Stephan A. Douglas failed to get the votes needed for the nomination. The Democrats finally coalesced around Pierce, who left the convention with an almost unanimous vote. Pierce's greatest asset was that no one knew anything about him, and he had taken no strong positions on anything.

The Whig Convention was even more confused, disorganized, and depressing. Scott and Fillmore were almost even for more than forty ballots, with each candidate getting between 128 and 134 votes. Webster consistently had about 30 votes. Finally, on the fifty-third ballot, Fillmore dropped to 112, Webster to 21, and Scott won.

The convention balloting illustrates the enigma or the incompetence of Fillmore.[7] Whatever his ambivalence might have been about seeking the presidency in 1850, by early 1852 he was an active candidate, and he clearly hungered to run by the time of the convention. He was convinced that Scott's nomination would destroy the party and hand the White House to the Democrats. Fillmore lost the nomination because of his own secretary of state. On the first ballot, Fillmore had 133 votes, Scott had 131, and Webster had an anemic 29. Had Webster withdrawn in favor of Fillmore, he could have been nominated on any of the ballots from the second to the fifty-second. Fillmore had rescued Webster's career after his Seventh of March speech had made him anathema in his own state. He and Webster had worked together for two years, and earlier in their lives Fillmore had been Webster's protégé. Still, Fillmore was incapable of getting Webster to release his delegates. In fact, Fillmore did not even speak to Webster while the convention was in session. The result was a catastrophic convention that kept Fillmore from the nomination and left Scott an utterly crippled candidate. The historian Michael F. Holt describes the behavior of Fillmore and Webster as "surreal" and observes that "one wonders why they simply did not meet themselves for an hour or two to resolve the deadlock." Holt suggests that "mutual pride and Webster's resentment" explains the debacle. He correctly notes that Webster's "pride was monumental," and he felt betrayed by Fillmore.[8]

Certainly, Webster behaved egotistically and foolishly. He publicly denounced Fillmore and cursed him.[9] However absurd Webster's behavior was, Fillmore's was ultimately worse. He was, after all, the president of the United States and had the power to bring Webster to the table. Fillmore might easily have summoned his subordinate—the secretary of state—to the White House. Indeed, months before the convention Fillmore might have done this and ordered Webster to either withdraw from the race or leave the cabinet. Even as president, Fillmore lacked the leadership and fortitude to do this. He was either too stubborn, or too insecure, or both, to actually take charge of the situation. As he had throughout his presidency, when the situation called for leadership, Fillmore was unable to act.

Webster's role in blocking Fillmore's nomination is one of the great humiliations in American political history—a sitting cabinet member sabotaging his own president. Even more remarkable, Fillmore compounded his humiliation by keeping Webster in his cabinet after the convention. When Webster died in October, Fillmore appointed Edward Everett as secretary of state. Everett, of course, had promised to support Fillmore at the convention, but during the convention he failed to intervene on the president's behalf with the New England delegations that continued to support Webster, thereby depriving Fillmore of the nomination. Fillmore seemed determined to reward those who had prevented him from gaining the nomination.

The fall election was a Whig disaster. Pierce carried all but four states, although he won barely 50 percent of the popular vote. Scott won only about 43 percent of the vote, with the rest going to other candidates. The Free Soil Democrat, John P. Hale, who had been one of the defense attorneys in the Shadrach prosecutions, won more than 150,000 votes. This was a purely antislavery vote— and it was two and a half times greater than the Liberty Party vote in 1844. Fillmore had managed to make opposition to slavery into a more viable political movement.

After the convention Fillmore bided his time waiting for his term to end. In August 1852 Fillmore appointed his longtime friend Nathan Hall to the U.S. District Court for the Western District of New York. Hall remained a judge until his death on March 2, 1874, just six days before the death of his patron and friend Millard Fillmore.

In February 1853 Fillmore began to ship his belongings to Buffalo. The tragedy of his administration was over, but his personal tragedies were not. On March 30, less than a month after he left office, Abigail Fillmore died, apparently from a cold she caught while attending Pierce's inauguration. A year later, in July 1854, Fillmore's twenty-two-year-old daughter, Mary Abigail, who had often served as the official hostess in the White House, suddenly died.

. . .

In March 1855 Fillmore embarked on a classic grand tour, visiting England, Ireland, France, Germany, Italy, Turkey, and Egypt. He was received by Queen Victoria, who reportedly thought him the handsomest man she had ever met. He modestly declined to accept an honorary degree from Oxford University, claiming he should not accept a diploma in Latin because he could not read the language. No man, he later explained, "should accept a degree he cannot read."[10] On the Continent he was given a personal tour of Berlin by Alexander von Humboldt, the great German naturalist and explorer, and later met with King Friedrich Wilhelm IV of Prussia. In Rome he had an audience with Pope Pius IX. Fillmore planned to decline this meeting until he was assured that he would not have to kneel or kiss the pope's ring or hand. The grand tour was rejuvenating and fulfilling, and by all accounts Europeans were impressed by Fillmore's reserved modesty and ability to engage in diplomatic small talk with heads of state. The self-educated Fillmore, who was always fascinated with geography and history, was able to see places he had only read about.

The oddest part of this journey may have been his meeting with the pope. Throughout his political career, Fillmore had been hostile to Catholics, but he nevertheless could not resist meeting the head of the Roman Catholic Church. In 1856 Fillmore returned to politics and another presidential run. The political landscape had completely changed. While there were still officeholders who called themselves Whigs, the national party barely existed. Most northern Whigs had joined the new Republican Party, which was dedicated to stopping, once and for all, the spread of slavery into the territories. This party emerged in 1854 when a massive Democratic majority in Congress passed the Kansas-Nebraska Act, opening most of the remaining federal territories to slavery. This law was the logical result of the Compromise of 1850. The laws Fillmore had signed in 1850 had opened all of the new western territories to slavery, including those like Nevada and Utah that were north of the Missouri Compromise line. Four years later Congress obliterated the compromise line in all of the remaining unorganized territories, allowing slavery in what would later become the states of Kansas, Nebraska, Colorado, South Dakota, North Dakota, Wyoming, and Montana.

Conservative northern Whigs still opposed almost everything the Democrats stood for, but they could not possibly support the Republicans with their slogan of Free Soil, Free Labor, Free Speech, and Free Men. Nor could they support the party's presidential nominee, John C. Frémont, a strongly antislavery senator from California. Southern Whigs remained in a party that was moribund and virtually irrelevant.

Millard Fillmore, however, had found a new political home. On February 22, 1856, the American Party, more commonly called the Know-Nothing Party, nominated Fillmore without serious opposition. The party's slogan said it all: Americans Must Rule America. The platform called for a prohibition on Catholics holding office and requiring twenty-one years of continuous residence for naturalization of immigrants. The main thrust of the party was to stop the immigration of Catholics and to purge them from public life, but it was almost as hostile to non-Catholic immigrants as well. Fillmore endorsed the goals of the Know-Nothings because, as he told a leader of the party, "I have for a long time looked with dread and apprehension at the corrupting influence which the contest for the foreign vote is exciting upon our election." He argued that foreign-born voters were "corrupting the ballot box."[11]

In accepting the party's nomination, Fillmore had come full circle. He had started his political career in the Anti-Masonic Party, which saw a conspiracy of Freemasons who were going to destroy the soul of America. Most Anti-Masons eventually moved into the Whig Party. He ended his political career with another weird third party, which saw a Catholic and immigrant conspiracy destroying America's Anglo-Saxon Protestant soul. The core of that party was made up of conservative Whigs, like Fillmore, who hated abolitionists, feared foreigners, and just wanted the slavery problem to go away. Fillmore told Alexander H. H. Stuart that he believed the Know-Nothings offered "the only hope of forming a truly national party, which shall *ignore* the constant and disturbing agitation of slavery."[12] In September 1856 what was left of the Whig Party also nominated Fillmore, but that nomination was as irrelevant as the party itself. In the general election Fillmore won a respectable 875,000 popular votes, but he carried only Maryland with its 8 electoral votes. He carried 44 percent of the popular vote in the slave states, which represented what was left of the Whigs in that section. But in the North he ran a distant third, with just 13 percent of the vote.[13] James Buchanan, a doughface Democrat from Pennsylvania, with a plurality popular vote of 1.8 million, won twelve southern states, five northern states, and the election. The Republican candidate, the western hero John C. Frémont, won eleven northern states and 1.3 million popular votes.

After the 1856 election Fillmore, only fifty-six years old, returned to Buffalo, married a wealthy widow just a few years younger than he was, and purchased a large mansion. His only official job was as chancellor of the University of Buffalo, but he was the city's most famous citizen and lived with honor and some luxury. By 1860 Fillmore's political career was over, but as a voter and a prominent citizen he supported John Bell of Tennessee, the candidate of the Constitutional Union Party. This party opposed any discussion of slavery and campaigned by essentially promising to bring back the old politics that had existed before Fillmore's presidency. The vice presidential candidate was Fillmore's former secretary of state Edward Everett, the same man who had promised to support him for the 1852 nomination but in the end did nothing to help his candidacy. Once again, Fillmore was associated with a fringe third party, working for someone who had undermined his career.

The 1860 presidential election led to the election of a former Whig congressman, Abraham Lincoln, who would implement many of the programs Fillmore had supported. Fillmore's dream of a transcontinental railroad, which he was powerless to start while president, began under Lincoln. Like Fillmore, Lincoln supported internal improvements, a central banking system, and a higher tariff. Lincoln vowed to preserve the Union (something Fillmore had always wanted to do). Despite all of the things he and Lincoln agreed on, Fillmore did not vote for him. After the election, however, Fillmore sent Lincoln a cordial note of congratulations and pledged his support for the new administration. On their way to Washington, Abraham and Mary Todd Lincoln spent a night at Fillmore's mansion in Buffalo.

When the Civil War began, Fillmore organized a local militia company of elderly men as a volunteer home guard who symbolically supported the war effort. He helped raise $25,000 for the relief of wounded soldiers. But by 1863 Fillmore had little use for the war. He opposed emancipation and the enlistment of black troops. In 1864 Buffalo's first citizen was asked to speak at a fundraiser to support wounded soldiers. To the shock of his audience, Fillmore denounced the war effort in part for "desolating the fairest portion of our nation" and because it "loaded the country with enormous debt."[14] As he had done while president, Fillmore remained more concerned about the needs and goals of the South than the North and was utterly unwilling to condemn the southern slaveholding republic that was making war on the nation he once led. Sound, traditional Whig economics were more important to him than holding the Union together or ending slavery. He argued the war might have been avoided and suggested it was caused by "partisan prejudice, petty jealousies, malignant envy, and intriguing, selfish ambition." In Fillmore's mind the war was entirely the fault of the North and a few secessionist fanatics who had "deluded" and "seduced" the southerners into rebellion. He did not suggest that the war might have been rooted in slavery, the failure of the compromise measures he signed, and his own aggressive crusades against free blacks, fugitive slaves, and white abolitionists. He urged "clemency and kindness" to the Confederates but had nothing to say about their treason or their slaveholding. He offered nothing to the slaves and former slaves, many of whom were by this time serving in the U.S. Army. The *Buffalo Commercial Advertiser*, which had long been in league with Fillmore on issues of boosterism and economic development, called him a "Copperhead" (a northerner who sympathized with the Confederacy) who was no longer "entitled to the consideration due to the dignity of his personal character, and to the remembrance of the high official station he once held." Privately, the ex-president argued that Lincoln was leading the nation to "national bankruptcy and military despotism."[15]

In 1864 Fillmore voted for the Democrat George McClellan, who wanted peace at any price and who completely rejected emancipation. Fillmore had never worried about freeing slaves or protecting the rights of free blacks, and nothing had changed. To his neighbors he was a Copperhead and perhaps a traitor. This was surely unfair. While Fillmore opposed the Lincoln administration, hated emancipation, and was willing to allow the destruction of the Union, he did not make war against his own country and thus had not committed treason. But there was surely an irony here. As president, Fillmore tossed around the word "treason" when talking about abolitionists, Free Soilers, free blacks, and Whig opponents of the Fugitive Slave Act. He had personally intervened to ensure that more than forty men were indicted for treason, simply because they refused to act as slave catchers. Fortunately for Fillmore, the Lincoln administration was more circumspect in its use of treason prosecutions. Otherwise, the ex-president, who now denounced the war effort and opposed black freedom, might have found himself facing the same charges he so aggressively pushed on others.

After the war he resumed his role as a famous citizen of Buffalo, which in 1860 had become the tenth largest city in the nation. His fame and honor were diminished by his opposition to emancipation and his Copperhead past. But he was still a former president. He busied himself with the Buffalo Historical Society, the University of Buffalo, and various other civic endeavors. He was a good citizen of his city. He took another trip to Europe, lived well, and died at home on March 8, 1874, forgotten almost everywhere but in his adopted hometown, where he is buried.

. . .

Millard Fillmore's legacy includes some visionary ideas that he could not accomplish: pushing for a transcontinental railroad (which Abraham Lincoln would begin); opening Japan to American diplomacy and trade (which Franklin Pierce would complete); maintaining a dominant American presence in Hawaii (allowing William McKinley to annex the islands); and pushing for a Central American canal (which Theodore Roosevelt would initiate).

But on the central issues of the age his vision was myopic and his legacy is worse. He opened the West to slavery and destroyed the Missouri Compromise line. This total appeasement of the South only encouraged new demands for more land for slavery. His solution to the issue of slavery in the territories simply led to the Kansas-Nebraska Act in 1854 and further conflict in the West. He signed and aggressively—indeed fanatically—implemented the Fugitive Slave Act of 1850, which was arguably the most oppressive law in American history. He ran for president on a ticket that openly attacked foreigners, immigrants, and Catholics. In retirement, Fillmore opposed emancipation and campaigned for a peace that would have left millions of African Americans in chains. In the end, Fillmore was always on the wrong side of the great moral and political issues of the age: immigration, religious toleration, equality, and, most of all, slavery.

Notes

1: PORTRAIT OF A YOUNG MAN FROM NOWHERE

1. See, generally, John S. D. Eisenhower, *Zachary Taylor* (New York: Times Books, 2008), 132–36.
2. As the governor of the Indiana Territory, Harrison had lobbied to allow slavery in the territory and even brought some of his own slaves there. Paul Finkelman, *Slavery and the Founders: Race and Liberty in the Age of Jefferson*, 2nd ed. (Armonk, NY: M. E. Sharpe, 2001), 65–70.
3. Oath of the President in U.S. Constitution, Art. II, Sec. 1, Par. 8.
4. Fillmore's early life is detailed in Robert J. Rayback, *Millard Fillmore: Biography of a President* (Buffalo, NY: Buffalo Historical Society, 1959); and Robert J. Scarry, *Millard Fillmore* (Jefferson, NC: McFarland and Company, 2001).
5. Michael F. Holt, *The Rise and Fall of the American Whig Party: Jacksonian Politics and the Onset of the Civil War* (New York: Oxford University Press, 1999), 193.
6. Abraham Lincoln to Joshua F. Speed (Aug. 24, 1855), in Roy P. Basler, ed., *The Collected Works of Abraham Lincoln* (New Brunswick, NJ: Rutgers University Press, 1953), 2:320. See Angela Alexander, "'All Men Are Created Equal': Abraham Lincoln, Immigration, and Ethnicity," *Albany Government Law Review* 3 (2010): 803.
7. "General Order No. 11, December 17, 1862," in John Y. Simon, ed., *The Papers of Ulysses S. Grant* (Carbondale and Edwardsville: Southern Illinois University Press, 1979), vol. 7.

8. Abraham Lincoln to Albert G. Hodges, April 4, 1864, in Basler, *Collected Works of Abraham Lincoln*, 7:281.

9. Abraham Lincoln to Horace Greeley, August 22, 1862, in ibid., 5:388–89.

10. Kristin Hoganson, "Abigail Powers Fillmore," in Lewis L. Gould, ed., *American First Ladies: Their Lives and Legacies*, 2nd ed. (New York: Routledge, 2001), 100. She was also the first presidential wife to earn a salary—as a teacher—before her marriage. No other presidential wife would work outside the home before or after marriage until Eleanor Roosevelt.

11. Daniel Walker Howe, *The Political Culture of the American Whigs* (Chicago: University of Chicago Press, 1979), 57.

12. Ibid.

13. Paul Finkelman, *An Imperfect Union: Slavery, Federalism, and Comity* (Chapel Hill: University of North Carolina Press, 1981); *Lemmon v. The People*, 20 NY 562 (1860).

14. Paul Finkelman, "The Protection of Black Rights in Seward's New York," *Civil War History* 34 (1988): 211–34.

15. Holt, *Rise and Fall of the American Whig Party*, 193.

16. Ibid., 188.

17. Comprising most of central New York along the Erie Canal from just east of Utica to west of Rochester, this area was the heart of New York's abolitionist movement. It was called the "Burned-over District" because the "fires" of evangelical reform had "burned over" the region so many times. The region was home to many of the state's most important abolitionists and antislavery politicians, including Gerrit Smith, Frederick Douglass, Rev. Samuel May, Alvan Stewart, Myron Holley, Rev. Jermain Loguen, Beriah Green, and William H. Seward.

18. Holt, *Rise and Fall of the American Whig Party*, 193.

19. Rayback, *Millard Fillmore*, 156–59.

20. Millard Fillmore to Henry Clay, November 11, 1844, in Frank Severence, ed., *Millard Fillmore Papers*, 2 vols. (Buffalo: Buffalo Historical Society Publications, 1907), 2:267 (quoted in Rayback, *Millard Fillmore*, 160).

21. Rayback, *Millard Fillmore*, 162, quoting the *Buffalo Express*, October 2, 1846.

2: TEXAS, MEXICO, AND THE VICE PRESIDENCY

1. For a short account of Texas settlement and annexation, see Walter Nugent, *Habits of Empire: A History of American Expansion* (New York: Random House, 2008), 130–56.

2. Joint Resolution for Annexing Texas to the United States Approved March 1, 1845, *Statutes at Large*, vol. 5, 797–98. Cary Wintz, "Joint

Resolution of Congress for the Annexation of Texas," in Paul Finkelman, ed., *Milestone Documents of American History* (Dallas: Schlager
Group, 2008), 2:609–18.

3. Eisenhower, *Zachary Taylor,* 30.
4. John H. Schroeder, *Mr. Polk's War: American Opposition and Dissent,
   1846–1848* (Madison: University of Wisconsin Press, 1973), 7–9.
5. James K. Polk, "Message to the Senate and House of Representatives," May 11, 1846, in James D. Richardson, ed., *A Compilation of
   the Messages and Papers of the Presidents* (New York: Bureau of
   National Literature, 1897), 5:2287, quoted on 2288, 2291, 2292.
6. For a brief history of the war, see Eisenhower, *Zachary Taylor,* 43–72;
   and Nugent, *Habits of Empire,* 187–220. More generally, see Robert W.
   Johannsen, *To the Halls of Montezuma: The Mexican American War in
   the American Imagination* (New York: Oxford University Press, 1985).
7. Fillmore in the *Buffalo Express,* October 2, 1846, quoted in Rayback,
   Millard Fillmore, 162.
8. Ibid.
9. The politics of the first Wilmot vote are described in David M.
   Potter, *The Impending Crisis, 1848–1861* (New York: Harper and
   Row, 1976), 20–23.
10. The term "doughface" was one of great insult, meant to imply that
    northern politicians who supported the South and slavery had faces
    made of bread dough and their southern colleagues could shape
    them any way they wanted. By the time he left the White House,
    many northerners would consider Fillmore to be a classic doughface.
11. William M. Wiecek, *The Sources of Antislavery Constitutionalism in
    the America, 1760–1848* (Ithaca: Cornell University Press, 1977),
    60; Finkelman, *Slavery and the Founders,* 37–39, 148–49.
12. Finkelman, *Slavery and the Founders,* 37–80.
13. Abraham Lincoln, "A House Divided," Speech of June 16, 1858, in
    Basler, *Collected Works of Abraham Lincoln,* 2:461.
14. Harold M. Hyman and William M. Wiecek, *Equal Justice Under Law:
    Constitutional Development, 1835–1875* (New York: Harper and Row,
    1982), 86.
15. Holt, *Rise and Fall of the American Whig Party,* 260–61.
16. Charles Francis Adams, ed., *Memoirs of John Quincy Adams* (Phila-
    delphia: J. B. Lippincott, 1874) (Entry of June 3, 1828), 8:25, quoted
    in Paul Finkelman, "John McLean: Moderate Abolitionist and
    Supreme Court Politician," *Vanderbilt Law Review* 62 (2009): 525.
17. Paul Finkelman, "Story Telling on the Supreme Court: *Prigg v. Penn-
    sylvania* and Justice Joseph Story's Judicial Nationalism," in Dennis
    J. Hutchinson, David A. Strauss, and Geoffrey R. Stone, eds., *The
    Supreme Court Review, 1994* (Chicago: University of Chicago Press
    Journals, 1995), 247–94.

18. Taylor to Crittenden, March 23, 1847, quoted in Holt, *Rise and Fall of the American Whig Party,* 269.
19. Holt, *Rise and Fall of the American Whig Party,* 271.
20. In some ways, the 1848 nomination paralleled the 1952 Republican Convention. The party faithful favored Robert Taft, known as "Mr. Republican," and on the first ballot he had 500 votes while General Eisenhower—who like Taylor was a military hero with no party track record—had 595 votes. But a shift immediately occurred as delegates changed their votes, and Eisenhower gained the nomination. James T. Havel, *U.S. Presidential Candidates and the Elections: A Biographical and Historical Guide* (New York: Macmillan Library Reference, 1996), 2:173.
21. Ibid., 2:24.
22. Holt, *Rise and Fall of the American Whig Party,* 325–26.
23. Charles Sumner, "Union of Men of All Parties Against the Slave Power and the Extension of Slavery," Speech of June 28, 1848, in Charles Frisbie Hoar, ed., *The Complete Works of Charles Sumner* (Boston: Lee and Shepherd, 1900), 2:74, quoted on 88.
24. The discussion here and in the following paragraphs comes mostly from Michael Holt's magisterial history of the Whig Party, *Rise and Fall of the American Whig Party.*
25. This is wonderfully described in ibid., 328.
26. Havel, *U.S. Presidential Candidates and the Elections,* 2:24.
27. The vice presidency has remained a one-way ticket to oblivion, except for those who have succeeded a president after his death. After Martin Van Buren, in 1836, no sitting vice president would be elected president again until George H. W. Bush won in 1988. In addition to Van Buren and Bush, only one former vice president, Richard M. Nixon, would be elected president on his own.

3: A HEARTBEAT AWAY

1. This was the first of only four times when a former president has run for president. Three—Van Buren (1848), Fillmore (1856), and Theodore Roosevelt (1912)—ran on third-party tickets and lost. The fourth, Grover Cleveland, won, running as a Democrat in 1892 after he had been elected in 1884 and then lost the election in 1888, even though he had a majority of the popular vote.
2. Potter, *Impending Crisis,* 86.
3. Ibid.
4. At this time state legislatures elected U.S. senators. Direct election of senators did not come about until the ratification of the Seventeenth Amendment in 1913.
5. On the Ohio Black Law repeal, see Paul Finkelman, "The Strange

Career of Race Discrimination in Antebellum Ohio," *Case Western Reserve University Law Review* 55 (2004): 373–408.

6. One exception was Jackson's choice of Van Buren.

7. Quotations from Fillmore letters are in Scarry, *Millard Fillmore*, 132.

8. Fillmore to W. G. Sneathen, July 4, 1848, quoted in ibid; Fillmore to John Gayle, July 31, 1848, in Severence, *Fillmore Papers*, 2:279–80.

9. Rayback, *Millard Fillmore*, 196.

10. As best I can determine, up to this point every other future president had at least met his future vice president at the time of the nomination. But never before had such an obscure politician been elected vice president.

11. The only other presidents who held no political positions or offices before their election were Ulysses S. Grant and Dwight David Eisenhower. But, unlike Taylor, they were both commanding generals in long and complicated wars. As the sole lieutenant general and general in chief of all Union armies, Grant had enormous political experience during the Civil War dealing with Congress and the president. His promotion to full general in 1866 and his work during Reconstruction gave him even more political and administrative experience. Similarly, as general of the army and supreme allied commander during World War II and as NATO supreme commander after leaving the Columbia University presidency, Eisenhower had enormous political and diplomatic experience. Two other presidents also had no electoral experience, although they had held various public offices. William Howard Taft had served as a judge, cabinet member, and unelected territorial governor before running for president, and Herbert Hoover had been a cabinet officer and served in many other political positions.

12. Rayback, *Millard Fillmore*, 160.

13. The United States government would not provide an official residence for the vice president until 1974.

14. Elbert B. Smith, *The Presidencies of Zachary Taylor & Millard Fillmore* (Lawrence: University of Kansas Press, 1988), 59.

15. Millard Fillmore to James Brooks, May 24, 1852, in Severence, *Fillmore Papers*, 2:321, quoted on 323 (explaining two years after the fact that he had told Taylor he would support the bill). See also Holt, *Rise and Fall of the American Whig Party*, 522–23, who argues that Fillmore had not yet decided if he would support the omnibus bill or not.

16. Holt, *Rise and Fall of the American Whig Party*, 385–86; Basler, *Collected Works of Abraham Lincoln* 2:20–22. On Lincoln's lifelong desire to end slavery, see Paul Finkelman, "Lincoln, Emancipation and the Limits of Constitutional Change," in Dennis J. Hutchinson, David A. Strauss, and Geoffrey R. Stone, eds., *The Supreme Court Review, 2008* (Chicago: University of Chicago Press Journals, 2009), 349–87; and Paul Finkelman, "Lincoln and the Preconditions for

Emancipation: The Moral Grandeur of a Bill of Lading," in William A. Blair and Karen Fisher Younger, eds., *Lincoln's Proclamation: Race, Place, and the Paradoxes of Emancipation* (Chapel Hill: University of North Carolina Press, 2009), 13–44.

17. U.S. Constitution, Art. IV, Sec. 2, Par. 3. For a discussion of the passage of this law, see Finkelman, *Slavery and the Founders*, 3–36, 81–104.

18. Thomas D. Morris, *Free Men All: The Personal Liberty Laws of the North, 1780–1861* (Baltimore: Johns Hopkins University Press, 1974); Paul Finkelman, "States Rights North and South in Antebellum America," in Kermit Hall and James W. Ely Jr., eds., *An Uncertain Tradition: Constitutionalism and the History of the South* (Athens: University of Georgia Press, 1989), 125–58; Finkelman, "Protection of Black Rights in Seward's New York," 211–34. Three successive Maine governors—Robert Dunlap, Edward Kent, and John Fairfield— were involved in the dispute with Georgia.

19. "*Prigg v. Pennsylvania* and Northern State Courts: Anti-Slavery Use of a Pro-Slavery Decision," *Civil War History* 25 (1979): 5–35; Finkelman, "Story Telling on the Supreme Court," 247–94. Paul Finkelman, *Slavery in the Courtroom* (Washington, DC: Library of Congress, 1985).

20. Cong. Globe, 31st Cong., 1st Sess. 19 (1850): 244–52.

21. For a discussion of attempts to bring slaves into California, see Paul Finkelman, "The Law of Slavery and Freedom in California," *California Western Law Review* 17 (1981): 437–64.

22. David Potter, in a Pulitzer Prize–winning book, argued that the territorial settlement "contributed nothing to the strength of the 'slave power'" because the land was "already covered by the Missouri Compromise." Potter, *Impending Crisis*, 100. This is simply wrong as a matter of geography, since a huge portion of the Mexican Cession was north of the Missouri Compromise line.

23. David Potter incorrectly claimed that these were not "tangible advantages" to the South. Ibid.

24. "Congress shall have Power . . . to exercise exclusive Legislation in all Cases whatsoever, over such District . . . as may, by Cession of particular States, and the Acceptance of Congress, become the Seat of the government of the United States." U.S. Constitution, Art. I, Sec. 8.

25. Ibid.

26. Smith, *Presidencies of Zachary Taylor & Millard Fillmore*, 119–20.

27. Ibid., 141, 167.

28. Ibid.

4: THE NEW PRESIDENT

1. Scarry, *Millard Fillmore,* 154–55, 151–53.
2. For example, the famous Francis B. Carpenter oil painting (1864) of Lincoln reading the Emancipation Proclamation to his cabinet does *not* include Hannibal Hamlin, the vice president. Similarly, the Mathew Brady daguerreotype *President Taylor and His Cabinet* in the National Portrait Gallery (NPG76.53) does not include Fillmore.
3. It is worth remembering that Harry Truman had no knowledge of the Manhattan Project when he became president after Roosevelt's death.
4. Rayback, *Millard Fillmore,* 334, quoting Stuart.
5. Elbert B. Smith incorrectly asserts, with no evidence, that Corwin supported the Wilmot Proviso. Smith, *Presidencies of Zachary Taylor & Millard Fillmore,* 167.
6. Graham remained in the Whig Party until it collapsed and opposed secession in 1860 but then served in the Confederate Senate.
7. After World War II, the Departments of War and Navy were combined into the Department of Defense.
8. While Fillmore sought a unionist cabinet, Conrad, like Graham, would serve in the Confederate Congress.
9. Unlike the other cabinet members from future Confederate states, Stuart was not in the Confederate government.
10. John McLean, for example, served as postmaster general in the Monroe, Adams, and Jackson administrations, before Jackson put him on the Supreme Court. Similarly, President Obama kept Secretary of Defense Robert Gates in office, even though he was appointed by a president of a different party.
11. Fillmore might have argued that the Texas debt was similar to the Revolutionary War state bonds that the United States paid off under the programs of Secretary of the Treasury Alexander Hamilton. Such an argument would have strengthened a sense of federalism and national power in the South.
12. David Potter calls it "The Armistice of 1850," in a chapter by that title in Potter, *Impending Crisis,* chap. 2.
13. "Message to the Senate and House of Representatives, August 6, 1850," in Richardson, *Compilation,* 6:2605.
14. The issue of immigration is important, given Fillmore's long-standing alliances with nativists and his final run for the presidency on the ticket of the anti-Catholic, anti-immigrant Know-Nothing Party.
15. Message to the Senate and House of Representatives, August 6, 1850, in Richardson, *Compilation,* 6:2607.

16. Holt, *Rise and Fall of the American Whig Party*, 542.
17. Some southerners in fact were contemptuous of the willingness of northerners to participate in the return of fugitive slaves. While the law was being debated, one Kentuckian told Senator Salmon P. Chase that in the South "no man will voluntarily become a negro catcher" and that it would be a "gross insult" to ask a southern gentleman to do such a thing. Professional slave catchers were "held in public estimation only secondary to the professional Negro trader, and that is the lowest possible." Edgar Needham to Salmon P. Chase, February 9, 1850, Salmon P. Chase Papers, Library of Congress.
18. U.S. Constitution, Art. I, Sec. 9, Par. 2.
19. Joseph P. Thompson, *The Fugitive Slave Law: Tried by the Old and New Testaments* (New York: M. H. Newman & Co., 1850), 8, quoted in Paul Finkelman, "The Treason Trial of Castner Hanway," in Michal Belknap, ed., *American Political Trials*, 2nd ed. (Westport, CT: Greenwood, 1994), 80.
20. Smith, *Presidencies of Zachary Taylor & Millard Fillmore*, 200.
21. Rayback, *Millard Fillmore*, 252.
22. Holt, *Rise and Fall of the American Whig Party*, 533.
23. Ibid.
24. Cong. Globe, 31st Cong., 1st Sess. 19 (1850): 1660, 1806–7, 1810; *Journal of the Senate*, Sept. 16, 1850, 638. *Opinions of the Attorney General* 5, September 18, 1850, 254.
25. Fillmore to Daniel Webster, October 23, 1850, reprinted in Claude H. Van Tyne, *The Letters of Daniel Webster* (New York: McClure and Phillips, 1902), 436–37.
26. Ibid.
27. Ibid.
28. Ibid.

5: MANIFEST DESTINY AND A WHIG PRESIDENCY

1. John L. O'Sullivan, "Annexation," *United States Democratic Review*, July–August (1845): 5, reprinted in Ernesto Chávez, *The U.S. War with Mexico: A Brief History with Documents* (Boston: Bedford Books, 2008), 35–37.
2. Millard Fillmore, "First Annual Address," December 2, 1850, in Richardson, *Compilation*, 6:2613, quoted on 2615, 2626, 2620.
3. The "Northwest" here referred to the old Northwest Territory. For Fillmore, the Northwest was Minnesota, Wisconsin, Michigan, Ohio, Indiana, and Illinois.
4. Millard Fillmore, "Second Annual Message," December 2, 1851, Richardson, *Compilation*, 2666; and "An act making appropriations

for the improvement of certain harbors and rivers," Act of August 30, 1852, 10 Stat. 56.

5. Fillmore, "First Annual Message," 2621; "An act to establish a branch of the Mint of the United States in California," Act of July 3, 1852, 10 Stat. 11.

6. Morton Borden, *Jews, Turks, and Infidels* (Chapel Hill: University of North Carolina Press, 1984), 83.

7. Ibid., 83, 84; Millard Fillmore, "To the Senate of the United States," February 13, 1851; and Millard Fillmore "To the Senate of the United States," February 3, 1853, in Richardson, *Compilation*, 2635, 2723.

8. Borden, *Jews, Turks, and Infidels*, 82–94.

9. Scarry, *Millard Fillmore*, 189.

10. Steven Lubar, "In the Footsteps of Perry: The Smithsonian Goes to Japan," *The Public Historian* 17 (Summer 1995): 25; Smith, *Presidencies of Zachary Taylor & Millard Fillmore*, 225–26; George Feifer, *Breaking Open Japan: Commodore Perry, Lord Abe, and American Imperialism in 1853* (New York: Collier Books, 2006).

11. The term comes from the Spanish *filibustero* ("pirate"), which came from the Dutch *vrijbuiter* ("freebooter")—someone who takes loot or "booty" from someone else.

12. James McPherson, *Battle Cry of Freedom: The Civil War Era* (New York: Oxford University Press, 1988), 106.

13. "By the President of the United States: A Proclamation," April 25, 1851, in Richardson, *Compilation*, 2647–48.

14. Millard Fillmore, "To the Senate and House of Representatives," July 2, 1852 in Richardson, *Compilation*, 2692–93; "An Act for the relief of American citizens lately imprisoned and pardoned by the Queen of Spain," Act of Feb. 10, 1852, 10 Stat. 2; "An act to supply Deficiencies in Appropriations in Service for the fiscal Year ending the thirtieth of June, one thousand eight hundred and fifty-two," Act of July 21, 1852, 10 Stat. 15 at 21.

6: A COMPROMISED PRESIDENCY

1. Rayback, *Millard Fillmore*, 253.

2. Fillmore letters quoted in Scarry, *Millard Fillmore*, 132.

3. Fillmore to Daniel Webster, October 23, 1850, reprinted in Van Tyne, *Letters of Daniel Webster*, 436–37.

4. William P. Newman to Frederick Douglass, October 1, 1850, reprinted in C. Peter Ripley, ed., *The Black Abolitionist Papers*, vol. 4, *The United States, 1847–1858* (Chapel Hill: University of North Carolina Press, 1991), 61–67.

5. Robert E. McGlone, *John Brown's War Against Slavery* (New York: Cambridge University Press, 2009), 135–36.

6. Stanley Campbell, *The Slave Catchers: Enforcement of the Fugitive Slave Law, 1850–1860* (Chapel Hill: University of North Carolina Press, 1968), 115–16.

7. Ibid., 51.

8. Ibid., 199–207.

9. Fillmore to Daniel Webster, October 23, 1850, reprinted in Van Tyne, *Letters of Daniel Webster*, 436–37.

10. Frederick Douglass, "Let All Soil Be Free Soil," speech of Aug. 11, 1852, in Pittsburgh, in John Blassingame et al., eds., *The Frederick Douglass Papers*, Series One, *Speeches, Debates, and Interviews*, vol. 2, *1847–54* (New Haven: Yale University Press, 1982), 390.

11. American and Foreign Anti-Slavery Society, *The Fugitive Slave Bill: Its History and Unconstitutionality; With an Account of the Seizure and Ensalvement of James Hamlet, and His Subsequent Restoration to Liberty* (New York: W. Harned, 1850), 36; Finkelman, *Slavery in the Courtroom*, 85–86.

12. Fillmore to Webster, Oct. 23, 1850, in Severence, *Fillmore Papers*, 1:333–35.

13. Message to the Senate and House of Representatives, August 6, 1850, in Richardson, *Compilation*, 6:2605. Similarly, his response also contrasts with his refusal to stop filibusters who used the United States to invade Cuba or arrest them, despite their violations of American law.

14. Potter, *Impending Crisis*, 126; see also Holt, *Rise and Fall of the American Whig Party*, 608.

15. Millard Fillmore, "First Annual Address," December 2, 1850, in Richardson, *Compilation*, 6:2613, quoted on 2615, 2626, 2620.

16. Ibid., quoted on 2616.

17. Ibid., quoted on 2628.

18. Ibid., quoted on 2616 and 2628–29.

19. Holt, *Rise and Fall of the American Whig Party*, 612.

20. Ibid., 128.

21. This is traditionally called the Shadrach Rescue because at the time of his arrest his last name was never used and perhaps not known by most people.

22. Gary Collison, " 'This Flagitious Offense': Daniel Webster and the Shadrach Rescue Cases, 1851–1852," *New England Quarterly* 68 (Dec. 1995): 609–25; Finkelman, *Slavery in the Courtroom*, 86–88; Harold Schwartz, "Fugitive Slave Days in Boston," *New England Quarterly* 27 (June 1954): 191–212.

23. This is traditionally called the Jerry Rescue because at the time of his arrest his last name was never used. To this day there is some debate whether his full name was Jerry Henry or Jerry McHenry.

24. Leonard W. Levy, *The Law of the Commonwealth and Chief Justice Shaw* (Cambridge: Harvard University Press, 1957), 102.
25. Daniel Webster, *The Writings and Speeches of Daniel Webster*, 18 vols. (Boston: Little, Brown 1903), 13:408–28.
26. The discussion of the Christiana case comes from Finkelman, "Treason Trial of Castner Hanway," 77–95.
27. In the nineteenth century, Supreme Court justices rode circuit and presided over jury trials in the circuit court. Most of the northern Supreme Court justices thus dealt with fugitive slave cases, but ironically southern slaveholding justices never heard these cases.
28. Finkelman, "Treason Trial of Castner Hanway," 87.
29. Ibid., 91.
30. "By the President of the United States: A Proclamation," April 25, 1851, in Richardson, *Compilation*, 2647–48.
31. Rayback, *Millard Fillmore*, 334, quoting Stuart.

7: DEFEAT, FAILED RESURRECTION, AND RETIREMENT

1. Rayback, *Millard Fillmore*, 332–35.
2. Ibid., 335.
3. Ibid., 340.
4. Ibid., 338–39.
5. Ibid., 350.
6. Harrison, who was born into a slaveholding family, probably would have supported slavery but he died too soon to do much of anything. Van Buren had been pro-slavery, but less so than Fillmore and of course by 1848 he had become a Free Soiler.
7. See, generally, Holt, *Rise and Fall of the American Whig Party*, 717–25, for a detailed discussion of the balloting.
8. Ibid., 721–22.
9. Ibid., 722.
10. Scarry, *Millard Fillmore*, 270.
11. Fillmore to Isaac Newton, January 1, 1855, in Severence, *Fillmore Papers*, 2:347–49.
12. Fillmore to Alexander H. H. Stuart, quoted in Holt, *Rise and Fall of the American Whig Party*, 911.
13. In losing this election, Fillmore became the first man to ever hold the presidency and then lose in the only time he ran for the office. In 1976 Gerald Ford would achieve this distinction, such as it is, as well.
14. Fillmore speech quoted in Rayback, *Millard Fillmore*, 427.
15. Fillmore speech, *Commercial Advertiser*, and Fillmore letter, all quoted in ibid., 427–29.

Milestones

1800   Born in Cayuga County, New York, January 7, to Phoebe Millard and Nathaniel Fillmore.

1815   Apprenticed to wool mill.

1817   Joins private library.

1819   Attends local academy, meeting Abigail Powers; clerks for Judge Walter Wood.

1820   Teaches school; buys his way out of his mill apprenticeship; quits clerkship with Judge Wood.

1821–23   Moves with family to East Aurora, New York. Resumes law clerking in Buffalo.

1823   Admitted to practice in Buffalo; moves back to East Aurora and becomes solo practitioner.

1826   Marries Abigail Powers.

1828   Elected to first of three consecutive one-year terms in New York Assembly, elected each time as a candidate of the Anti-Masonic Party; son, Millard Powers Fillmore, is born.

1830   Reelected for the third time but moves from East Aurora to Buffalo.

1831   Drafts bill ending imprisonment for debt, which passes in April.

1832	Daughter, Mary Abigail, born. Practices law in Buffalo. Elected to Congress as an Anti-Mason.
1833	On December 2 takes his seat in the new Congress.
1834	Returns to Buffalo, forms new law firm with former clerk Nathan K. Hall as partner; declines to run for reelection to Congress.
1836	Adds third lawyer to his firm, Solomon Haven. In November wins congressional seat running as a Whig. Reelected in 1838 and 1840; in last term is elected chairman of the Ways and Means Committee.
1842	Guides Whig tariff bill through House. Declines to run for reelection.
1844	Seeks vice presidential nomination at Whig Convention but loses. Runs for governor as a Whig and loses by 10,000 votes; the Whig presidential candidate, Henry Clay, loses the state by only 5,000 votes. In this campaign Fillmore refuses to take an antislavery stand on Texas annexation and openly seeks support of anti-Catholic nativists.
1846	Becomes chancellor of the University of Buffalo, a position he holds for the rest of his life.
1847	Wins election as comptroller of New York. He is the first elected comptroller in the state, chosen under the new state constitution.
1848	Elected vice president, running with Zachary Taylor on the Whig ticket.
1849	Takes office as vice president on March 5.
1850	Presides over Senate during the major debates over the Compromise of 1850. In early July tells President Taylor he will vote for the compromise if he has to break a tie. President Taylor dies on July 9; Fillmore takes oath of office the following day. Immediately removes all members of the cabinet, the only successor president to do so. Between September 9 and September 20 Fillmore signs the various bills that are the components of the Compromise of 1850. On September 26 the Fillmore administration begins

aggressive enforcement of the Fugitive Slave Act with the secret arrest in New York City of James Hamlet.

Delivers his first annual address to Congress on December 2, in which he condemns opposition to the new compromise laws.

1851   The Fillmore administration, led by Secretary of State Daniel Webster, arranges for the arrest of the fugitive slave Jerry in Syracuse, New York, but he is rescued from federal custody that night.

Fugitive slaves in Christiana, Pennsylvania, resisting capture, kill a Maryland slave owner. Fillmore personally orders federal prosecutors in Pennsylvania to seek treason indictments and personally consults with the U.S. attorney in Pennsylvania for what becomes the largest treason prosecution in the entire history of the United States. These trials end in outright acquittals.

Fillmore warns Americans not to participate in filibustering ventures against Cuba but then uses federal funds and diplomatic intervention to bring back Americans captured by the Spanish.

Fillmore signs and sends to the Senate a treaty with Switzerland that allows for discrimination against Jews. Senate rejects treaty and demands changes.

Secretary of State Webster announces that he will seek the Whig presidential nomination in 1852.

1852   In June, after three days of balloting, Fillmore loses the Whig presidential nomination to General Winfield Scott. Webster refuses to release his delegates to vote for Fillmore, thus giving the nomination to Scott. Fillmore retains Webster in his cabinet.

In the November election Scott is swamped by the Democratic candidate, Franklin Pierce. After the election Fillmore sends Commodore Matthew Perry to Japan to open that nation to American diplomacy and trade.

1853   Fillmore sends Swiss treaty back to the Senate with language that still allows for religious discrimination.

On March 4 Fillmore leaves office and returns to Buffalo. On March 30, his wife, Abigail, dies.

1854   Daughter Mary Abigail Fillmore dies.

1855–56   Fillmore visits Europe and Egypt on a grand tour. Meets Queen Victoria, King Friedrich Wilhelm IV of Prussia, and Pope Pius IX.

1856   While in Europe, Fillmore receives the nomination of the anti-Catholic, anti-immigrant Know-Nothing Party. In May he accepts the nomination while in Paris. Arrives home in June and is defeated in November, carrying just one state, Maryland.

1858   Fillmore marries Caroline C. McIntosh, a wealthy widow from Albany. They move to Buffalo, where Fillmore builds a large mansion.

1860   Supports Constitutional Union Party for the presidency.

1861   President-elect Lincoln stays with Fillmore on his way to Washington, but Fillmore does not become a Republican or a supporter of the president. When Civil War begins, he organizes a home guard of elderly men and raises money for soldiers' relief.

1862   Is a founder of the Buffalo Fine Arts Academy and a founder and first president of the Buffalo Historical Society.

1863   Opposes Lincoln's emancipation policy. Many in Buffalo consider him a Copperhead and perhaps a traitor as he advocates ending the war without ending slavery or preserving the Union.

1864   Opposes Lincoln's reelection and supports the Democratic candidate, George B. McClellan.

1866   Tours Europe with his wife. Meets with President Andrew Johnson and endorses his antiblack Reconstruction policies.

1867–74   Holds various civic posts as president of the Buffalo Club and president of the Buffalo General Hospital; retains his position as chancellor of the University of Buffalo.

1874   Dies on March 8 in his home, after suffering his second stroke in less than a month.

Selected Bibliography

American and Foreign Anti-Slavery Society. *The Fugitive Slave Bill: Its History and Unconstitutionality; With an Account of the Seizure and Ensalvement of James Hamlet, and His Subsequent Restoration to Liberty.* New York: W. Harned, 1850.

Basler, Roy P. *The Collected Works of Abraham Lincoln.* New Brunswick, NJ: Rutgers University Press, 1953.

Borden, Morton. *Jews, Turks, and Infidels.* Chapel Hill: University of North Carolina Press, 1984.

Campbell, Stanley W. *The Slave Catchers: Enforcement of the Fugitive Slave Law, 1850–1860.* Chapel Hill: University of North Carolina Press, 1968.

Chamberlin, Ivory, and Thomas M. Foote. *Biography of Millard Fillmore.* Buffalo, NY: Thomas and Lathrops, 1856.

Chávez, Ernesto. *The U.S. War with Mexico: A Brief History with Documents.* Boston: Bedford Books, 2009.

Collison, Gary. "'This Flagitious Offense': Daniel Webster and the Shadrach Rescue Cases, 1851–1852," *New England Quarterly* 68 (Dec. 1995): 609–25.

Crawford, John E. *Millard Fillmore: A Bibliography.* Westport, CT: Greenwood Press, 2002.

Eisenhower, John S. D. *Zachary Taylor.* New York: Times Books, 2008.

Feifer, George. *Breaking Open Japan: Commodore Perry, Lord Abe, and American Imperialism in 1853.* New York: Collier Books, 2006.

Feller, Daniel. "A Requiem for Whigs," on H-Net, https://www.H-Net.org/reviews/showtev.php?id=3652.

Finkelman, Paul. *An Imperfect Union: Slavery, Federalism, and Comity.* Chapel Hill: University of North Carolina Press, 1981.

———. "The Protection of Black Rights in Seward's New York." *Civil War History* 34 (1988): 211–34.

———. *Slavery in the Courtroom.* Washington, DC: Government Printing Office, 1985.

———. *Slavery and the Founders: Race and Liberty in the Age of Jefferson.* 2nd ed. Armonk, NY: M. E. Sharpe, 2001.

———. "States' Rights North and South in Antebellum America," in Kermit Hall and James W. Ely Jr., eds., *An Uncertain Tradition: Constitutionalism and the History of the South,* 125–58. Athens: University of Georgia Press, 1989.

———. "Story Telling on the Supreme Court: *Prigg v. Pennsylvania* and Justice Joseph Story's Judicial Nationalism," in Dennis J. Hutchinson, David A. Strauss, and Geoffrey R. Stone, eds., *The Supreme Court Review, 1994.* Chicago: University of Chicago Press Journals, 1995.

———. "The Treason Trial of Castner Hanway," in Michal Belknap, ed., *American Political Trials.* 2nd ed., 77–95. Westport, CT: Greenwood, 1994.

Hamilton, Holman. *Prologue to Conflict: The Crisis and Compromise of 1850.* Lexington: University of Kentucky Press, 1964.

Hoar, Charles Frisbie, ed. *The Complete Works of Charles Sumner.* Boston: Lee and Shepherd, 1900.

Hoganson, Kristin. "Abigail Powers Fillmore," in Lewis L. Gould, ed., *American First Ladies: Their Lives and Legacies.* 2nd ed., 100–102. New York: Routledge, 2001.

Holt, Michael F. *The Rise and Fall of the American Whig Party: Jacksonian Politics and the Onset of the Civil War.* New York: Oxford University Press, 1999.

Howe, Daniel Walker. *The Political Culture of the American Whigs.* Chicago: University of Chicago Press, 1979.

Hyman, Harold M., and William M. Wiecek. *Equal Justice Under Law: Constitutional Development, 1835–1875.* New York: Harper and Row, 1982.

Johannsen, Robert W. *To the Halls of Montezuma: The Mexican American War in the American Imagination.* New York: Oxford University Press, 1985.

Levy, Leonard W. *The Law of the Commonwealth and Chief Justice Shaw.* Cambridge: Harvard University Press, 1957.

Lubar, Steven. "In the Footsteps of Perry: The Smithsonian Goes to Japan," *The Public Historian* 17 (Summer 1995): 25.

McPherson, James M. *Battle Cry of Freedom: The Civil War Era.* New York: Oxford University Press, 1988.

Morris, Thomas D. *Free Men All: The Personal Liberty Laws of the North, 1780–1861*. Baltimore: Johns Hopkins University Press, 1974.

Nugent, Walter. *Habits of Empire: A History of American Expansion*. New York: Random House, 2008.

Potter, David. *The Impending Crisis, 1848–1861*. Completed and edited by Don E. Fehrenbacher. New York: Harper and Row, 1976.

Rayback, Robert. *Millard Fillmore: Biography of a President*. Buffalo, NY: Buffalo Historical Society, 1959.

Remini, Robert. *At the Edge of the Precipice: Henry Clay and the Compromise That Saved the Union*. New York: Basic Books, 2010.

Richardson, James D. *A Compilation of the Messages and Papers of the Presidents*. New York: Bureau of National Literature, 1897.

Scarry, Robert J. *Millard Fillmore*. Jefferson, NC: McFarland and Company, 2001.

Schroeder, John H. *Mr. Polk's War: American Opposition and Dissent, 1846–1848*. Madison: University of Wisconsin Press, 1973.

Schwartz, Harold. "Fugitive Slave Days in Boston," *New England Quarterly* 27 (June 1954): 191–212.

Severence, Frank. *Millard Fillmore Papers*. 2 vols. Buffalo, NY: Buffalo Historical Society Publications, 1907.

Smith, Elbert B. *The Presidencies of Zachary Taylor & Millard Fillmore*. Lawrence: University of Kansas Press, 1988.

Van Tyne, Claude H. *The Letters of Daniel Webster*. New York: McClure and Phillips, 1902.

Webster, Daniel. *The Writings and Speeches of Daniel Webster*. 18 vols. Boston: Little, Brown, 1903.

Wiecek, William M. *The Sources of Antislavery Constitutionalism in America, 1760–1848*. Ithaca, NY: Cornell University Press, 1977.

Wintz, Cary. "Joint Resolution of Congress for the Annexation of Texas," in Paul Finkelman, ed., *Milestone Documents of American History*, vol. 2, 609–18. Dallas: Schlager Group, 2008.

Acknowledgments

In the late 1820s and early 1830s and then again in the late 1840s, Millard Fillmore lived in Albany, initially as a member of the New York legislature and then as the first elected state comptroller. In 2008 his specter moved back to Albany, residing in my office at Albany Law School and simultaneously (as only a specter can do) in my home office. With him were books, articles, and collections of his papers, gathered by Bob Emery, Colleen Ostiguy, Colleen Smith, and Mary Wood, all members of the wonderful library staff of Albany Law School. My administrative assistant, Fredd Brewer, was, as always, enormously helpful, patient, and good-humored in finding material online and keeping track of seemingly endless amounts of paper. My research assistants, Reannon Froehlich and Lynn Nolan, helped sort through the material and ferret out more information about our thirteenth president. The staff of the American Antiquarian Society, particularly James D. Moran and the organization's president, Ellen S. Dunlap, found some rare newspaper stories about Fillmore and photographs of him. A. J. Aiseirithe, an editor of the Papers of Abraham Lincoln at the Library of Congress, helped me locate material relating to Fillmore and Abraham Lincoln. Jean Brown, the executive director of the Chicago Federal Executive Board, provided me with a wonderful opportunity to speak before the board about Fillmore and presidential leadership. Harvey Bennett of Mathew Bennett International and Scott Wieduwilt of Schuyler Rumsey, Inc., helped me sort out the complexities of mail and postage to the West under Fillmore. I greatly appreciate the time these experts offered to someone in a very different field than their own. Ablin (Abbie) Kowalewski at the Office of the Historian of the U.S. House of Representatives helped sort out when exactly the fugitive slave bill reached Fillmore's desk. The following friends and colleagues, in no particular order, helped me gather information and find obscure materials, discussed some of the issues with me, or read portions of the book: Simon Stern, R. B. Bernstein, James Oakes, Diane L. Barnes, Abraham R. Wagner, William M. Wiecek, Jeff Forret, Victoria Bernhardt, John Quist, Martin Hershock, Helen Knowles, Gillian Berchowitz, James Folts, John Kukla, Lisa K. Jensen, Dan Feller, and Fred I. Greenstein.

The opportunity to write this book was made possible by my agent, John W. Wright, who takes great care of his authors. I am enormously grateful to John for his support and encouragement. Paul Golob at Times Books was the perfect editor: smart, understanding, prodding (in the best ways), and a superb stylist. Arthur M. Schlesinger Jr. was the first general editor of the American Presidents series, and the series will be just one more lasting tribute to his innumerable contributions to our knowledge of American history, as well as his own contributions to the shaping of American history. I was deeply honored that he asked me to write for the series, but sadly he passed away before I could work with him. Sean Wilentz, the series' current general editor, has been very helpful in pointing me toward some aspects of Fillmore's career and pushing me to think harder about Fillmore's place in American politics. Emi Ikkanda, in Paul Golob's office, was enormously helpful in the final production of the book, as was Christopher O'Connell in the Henry Holt production department. This is a better book because of all their efforts.

Once Fillmore came to visit, he became a part of the family. My son, Isaac, regularly asked how Millard was doing, and when he might change his first name to something less odd. My daughter, Abby, read the final manuscript and my wife, Byrgen, read an early draft and the final page proofs. The book is better because of their input. I have dedicated this book to my oldest college friend, Abe Wagner, a fine scholar in his own right. Abe hails from Buffalo and has spent much of his life in government service, but otherwise he does not have very much in common with Millard.

Index